DATE

THE PUBLIC COMMISSION OF THE UNIVERSITY

THE PUBLIC COMMISSION OF THE UNIVERSITY

THE ROLE OF THE COMMUNITY OF SCHOLARS
AN INDUSTRIAL, URBAN, AND CORPORATE SOCIETY

JOHN F. A. TAYLOR

1981
NEW YORK UNIVERSITY PRESS
NEW YORK *and* LONDON

Library of Congress Cataloging in Publication Data

Taylor, John Francis Adams.
The public commission of the university.

Includes bibliographical references and index.
1. Higher education and state—United States.
2. Universities and colleges—United States—
Political aspects.   3. College teachers—Legal
status, laws, etc.—United States.   I. Title.
LC173.T39   378.73   81-2761
ISBN 0-8147-8165-9   AACR2

To E. F. T.

CONTENTS

PREFACE

The Public Commission of the University is a special application of the general theory of covenants set forth in my book, *The Masks of Society*.

I gratefully acknowledge the criticisms as well as the sustaining encouragements of my friends Madison Kuhn, Frederic Reed, and Truman Morrison.

The chapter entitled "Politics and the Neutrality of the University" appeared in December 1973 in the Winter issue of the *AAUP Bulletin* (Copyright © 1973 by *AAUP Bulletin*); it is reprinted by permission of the Editor. The lines from T. S. Eliot's "Gerontion," in *Collected Poems, 1909–1962* (New York: Harcourt Brace Jovanovich, Inc., 1962), are quoted by permission of the publisher.

J. F. A. T.

Okemos
October 8, 1980

INTRODUCTION

Education is in every season the portrait of the generation that produces it. The portrait varies; inevitably it must vary, if the education would be honest. But the patrimony of the society, the shared covenant that binds the generations together and makes them to be, in spite of their differences, of one house and progeny—this patrimony remains, and to meet it is to discover an intimate inward side of the human character that is otherwise inaccessible to us. Normally, we meet it only when, as in our times, its tenancy has been challenged.

When in the very season of the birth of the university, armed with all of the massive erudition of his contemporaries, Peter Abelard wrote that by doubting we are led to inquiry and by inquiry to truth, his fellow guildsmen either flocked to his banner or took up arms against him. Every man among them was obliged to follow or to stand opposed, for all were at once aware that a new path had been announced. A distinction was permitted between truth and doctrine, and all alike perceived that the question raised by Abelard was an unconcealed assault upon their ordinary patterns of inheritance. The matter at issue was not the credibility of this or that belief but the constitution of their community, their relations to each other in the free search for truth and its free exposition. Abelard asked: What are the conditions of consent that are essential to a free community of inquiry? What are the terms under which, if opinions are divided, any belief can be claimed to have rational authority?

That was the question that Abelard's contemporaries heard. Nor could anyone who understood the question remain neutral concerning the resolution that was to be made of it. Abelard's meaning was a shaking of the foundations of inquiry itself, the unsettling proposition, dangerous to every inherited formula, that only that is worthy of belief which is capable of withstanding any doubt that a free criticism might raise against it. And this (though Abelard professed that he would not contradict Saint Paul in order to be a philosopher, or desert Christ in order to be Aristotle himself) was the identifiable voice of the university.

The university will in every generation appear to deny more than it affirms. Inevitably it introduces into the work of thought the deranging reflection that truth is not what we start with but what we labor after. Abelard's purpose in doubting is constructive inquiry. His object is not to annihilate faith but to eliminate error. He doubts as Descartes and Kant after him will doubt, and as the university in every season will continue always to doubt, as a point of *method.* We begin with our beliefs, and our beliefs are in conflict. The problem is to know how, without foreknowledge of nature, to discriminate among contending beliefs in a single community of inquiry. We resolve the problem by a social covenant. We agree, in advance of all argument, on rules of due process that are to govern the argument itself. In short, we oblige ourselves to a common understanding of the meaning of proof and evidence. No belief may be accounted true which cannot maintain itself, by due process of argument, in an open community of inquiry. The argument thereby becomes independent of the disputants, and the disputants consent to be bound by it, wherever it may lead and by whomsoever it may be advanced or spoken.

The principle of an open community of scholarship, first clearly announced in the twelfth century, remains still to be explored in the twentieth. In the twentieth century it has become the key to any understanding of our moral predicament.

By "the public commission of the university" I mean the public commission of universities generally, not of public universities only. Assuredly I intend the latter: they constitute 63 percent of the American system. But the statutory distinction between the public and the private university is one of the carefully fostered illusions of our society. The private universities in America are no longer private except in legal ritual. During the Vietnam war, Princeton privately maintained only 28 percent of its total operation; Massachusetts Institute of Technology not more than 12 percent. This residual privacy enables them to preserve an outward semblance of privileged self-direction that is consistent with their traditions. But they are as little immune to the corporate thrust of American society as the manifestly public institutions.

I would moreover be understood to speak of the public commission of the university, not of the plural local establishments into which the university is divided. The scattered establishments of the university—for example, Harvard, Johns Hopkins, California—interest me only as they contribute to the shared purposes of the community of scholars, and I reserve the term "university" to name the corporate undertaking of this community. The community of scholars subdivides itself, according to the special demands of time and place, into a plurality of universities, colleges, institutes, and schools of advanced studies. But all such establishments claim to be party to the one community of scholars,[1] all alike claim to enact its general commission, in the practice of the higher learning both here and abroad.

What must the public commission of the university be?

What must be the relation of the university to society, and of scholars to each other, if the community of scholars is to bring knowledge to bear on the problems of our social condition?

I propose in these pages to examine the place of the university in twentieth-century society. Scholarship was once a private calling; it has become in modern America a *de facto* public office—what some have described as a fourth branch of government—in the American commonwealth. The modern commission of the university is in part determined by the venerable tradition from which it inherits in an unbroken succession from the Middle Ages. But it is determined also and no less by the new actualities of our own season,

> . . . by such unforeseen establishments as the marriage of science and government in the National Science Foundation and the National Endowment for the Humanities,
> . . . by the dispensations of the United States Supreme Court on academic freedom, the democratic process and the American Constitution,
> . . . by the rise of the professions as anarchic enclaves in the body politic,
> . . . by the substitution of collective bargaining for the collegiality of scholars,
> . . . by the confusion of tenure with job security,
> . . . by the intimations of an objective human covenant implicit in the demand for general education.

All of these developments originate beyond the university; all modify its pattern and influence its performance; together they disclose the magnitude of the university's involvement in our public life. And it is this transformation of the office of the university in our public life that I mean to study.

The conception of an intellectual commonwealth in which knowledge is sought after for its own sake needs no defense among the practicing scholars who are its celebrants. For them the idea of a commonwealth of learning is the rule and sufficient charter of their community. For society beyond the university, however, it is no such thing. The community of scholars exercises a privilege, not a right; and anyone who would understand the modern university is obliged to deal with the social and political and economic structures that lie beyond it and limit it, and inevitably determine the real conditions of its possibility, in the public life. Society will of its own motion license the benefits of science in uses which it understands; but of the free commission of the university, of the conditions essential to an open community of inquiry that diffuses its benefits gratuitously beyond the limits of the nation which has sponsored it and underwritten its costs, society understands very little and is prepared to license almost nothing. There is no major institution whose internal covenant is so little apprehended, or whose external relations—whose relations to government, to law, to the labor market, to international agencies—are so little reflected on, even by the scholars who are themselves party to these relations. An examination of these relations is today most urgently needed. Scholars have failed to communicate their conception of scholarship as the exercise of a public trust; therefore, in the general understanding, the public commission of the university has been reduced to the private enterprise of a profession.

The university exercises three distinguishable public functions that are proper to it: first, the function of *basic research*, by which its knowledge is gained and systematized; second, the function of *intellectual tradition*, by which its technical commission is handed on and renewed; third, the function of *education*, by which the moral commission of our larger society is comprehended, cultivated, and preserved.

Basic research is the pathfinding work of creative imagination and patient intellect. Its materials are drawn from the public world; its performances belong to the laboratory and the study, to the frontiers of assumption at which all problems remain open and all solutions provisional. In the American commonwealth the cultivation of the understanding is never entirely divorced from the pursuit of utility—at least never for very long. The alliance of science with public policy carries with it, for the larger purposes of the university, dangers as well as benefits. The basic commissions of scholarship are subordinated, sometimes blindly, to the accidents of government and society. The fact remains that no nation in history has expended upon the advancement of knowledge an equal measure of its energy, genius, or wealth. In 1964 America's investment in research (mission oriented as well as basic) rose to 3 percent of the gross national product of the richest economy in all the world.

The second function of the university, the function of intellectual tradition, belongs to the graduate faculties. Intellectual tradition is the sustaining foundation of the professions. Its purpose is twofold: to fund the knowledge of the accomplished sciences and to train the next generation of professionals to receive it. The graduate schools provide for the systematic tranfer of knowledge, sometimes by inadvertence even for its increase. But the distinctive and peculiar function of the graduate schools consists in transmitting, from generation to generation, the specialized norms that are implicit in professional practice. The education of a professional is made perfect, not by a consummation of knowledge, but by an understanding of the boundaries of professional authority.

For so long as the work of the university was restricted to basic research and intellectual tradition, its performances were, if socially limited, at least always socially manifest. Its commission was to set free the critical intellect and to educate professionals, the scientists and scholars of its own house. Within this limited commission it knew well enough how to perpetuate itself, transmitting the covenant of the scientist and the scholar, uniting their generations in one community of research and exchange.

But suppose that specialized and technical commission to be expanded; suppose the university to be charged (as in our day it is charged) with the task of educating the society beyond it, not only the rising generation of professionals, but the supporting society out of which they have come.

Epicurus counted it a piece of extraordinary good fortune that he came to philosophy, as he said, "undefiled by education." Had he been more carefully educated according to the patterns of his contemporaries, he would have asked safer questions and given safer answers. Especially would he have avoided the question his contemporaries most needed to hear, namely, What is the education proper to a human being? Nowadays, in the design of the modern curriculum, the university confronts the same question expressed with the same enigmatic generality. We do not ask to know the education of a lawyer, or of a medical physician, or of an engineer, or of a doctor of philosophy. We ask to know, quite simply, What is the education of a human being? And before that unpretentious question we are, like Epicurus' contemporaries, frankly baffled. The education of a technician is a calculable problem about which, among technicians, we may expect to find a reasonable measure of professional agreement. But the education of a human being is an ambiguous commission about which, among technicians, there is no agreement, professional or philosophical. In all of those connections in which human society is divided against itself, in all connections in which its premises are unworked or unrecovered or contradictory or obscure, we suffer a moral arrest of the most radical sort. The covenant of our society is confused, and our ordinary standards of criticism fluctuate. Therefore we leave education to the accidents of informal election or formal distribution. In either case, in reliance upon the ultimate wisdom of uninstructed preference, we desert our young. We desert our young as surely as we would desert them if we left medicine to the butcher, the baker, and the candlestick maker on the ground that they are all interested in health.

All the university can offer in any of its functions is criticism. That is why, before the unlimited commission of general education, it hesitates. Its reluctance to concern itself with partisanships that are alien to the neutral commissions of research and transmission is as old as the Lyceum and the Platonic Academy. In the Middle Ages, before the rise of the university in the cathedral schools of the twelfth century, the monastery cultivated the same withdrawal and sought, by a division of labor that allied the pen with the hoe, to make its enterprise self-subsistent and insular. In despair of the ways of the larger society, the monastery cloistered its moral commission, labored for the glory of God, and contracted upon itself. Let no one disparage it. The monastic *reculer pour mieux sauter* was one of the great conserving acts of renunciation and service in human history. The monastic principle of seclusion and withdrawal is, however, denied to the modern university. The modern university does not support itself; it has never professed to do so; and the secular society that supports it is indisposed to allow to it an unqualified autonomy. A secular society refuses to regard its own walks as profane; therefore it refuses to regard scholarship as an absolute office. That is why the educational function of the university is so perennially a problem. No university can make out its claim to support in separation from the integral life of society. Yet neither can it, without renouncing its claim to support, take its color from the uncritical routines of the society it serves.

The modern university is in the world; it is forbidden to be also of it. Its technical resources make it the most powerful agency for good or evil in the world today. Were its knowledge ever to become the monopoly of any nation or faction, that nation or faction would command mankind. Were its knowledge to be in one stroke extinguished, the nations of the earth would be reduced to a common sordid penury which surpasses any that we either know or can begin to imagine. But in the function of education, in the one function in which its critical powers are most vitally needed, the modern university is perfectly faceless. It has been so far drawn into the turbulent divisions of the social current that it is in danger of losing, and in some quarters has already lost, its capacity to communicate our social covenant. Powerful in division, it is without authority in peace. It has become, in spite of our labors, the modern version of Pilate's shrug. Therefore we would do well to look at it, to examine the conditions that are essential to it, lest we lose it, in fact as in thought, in dumb ignorance of its idea.

Rousseau professed, in studying the normative conditions of human community, to take men as they are, and institutions as they might be. I do very much the same thing. I define the commission of the university in any season and ask what conditions are necessary if it would perform its commission in ours, that is, in the context of government, foundations, anarchic professions, collective bargaining, and assaults on academic freedom.

NOTES

1. The membership of the community of scholars goes beyond the university narrowly so called. The community of scholars includes the independent college (Swarthmore, Mount Holyoke, Oberlin, Pomona) and the scientific institute (The Institute for Advanced Study, in Princeton); it includes the private scholar who labors without office or subsidy; it includes persons performing the investigations sponsored by the great private foundations (Carnegie, Rockefeller, Ford, Guggenheim); in some cases it includes persons working in industrial research laboratories and in government offices.

1.

POLITICS AND THE NEUTRALITY OF THE UNIVERSITY

1. INTELLECTUAL INDIVIDUALISM AND SOCIAL RESPONSIBILITY

In June 1968, in ceremonies held at the Cathedral of Saint John the Divine in New York City, the late Richard Hofstadter was called upon to deliver Columbia University's commencement address. He was addressing his own university, and he spoke, as everyone who heard him knew, in the profane and ruinous aftermath of a crisis that had shaken its foundations, suspended its scholarship, and thrown doubt upon the validity of its enterprise. Serious men, informed and cultivated men, men of infinitely subtle capacity and supple art, had discovered to their consternation that their community which no one had thought to question was in fact a delusion which no one chose to defend. Only their divisions were demonstrable, and events had not failed to afford the demonstration. Driven by a succession of bitter calamities, its buildings occupied, its faculty disorganized, its students in turbulent and open revolt, Columbia University had been compelled, before an astonished world, to close its doors.

"No one," said Hofstadter, "is authorized to speak for [the modern university]." The university is the "citadel of intellectual individualism," the one institution in modern society that makes independence of thought an obligation. In its neutral assembly all competent voices must be heard, and all who are loyal to it labor to assure that in fact these voices are heard, that no dissenting voice is ever denied a proper hearing. The university is therefore in principle forbidden to embrace the political partisanships of any of its members. "A university is firmly committed to certain basic values of freedom, rationality, inquiry, discussion, and to its own internal order; but it does not have corporate views on public questions." [1]

Those unadorned sentences are the distillation of an old and very proud tradition. They preserve Columbia's best part—its obligatory detachment, its freedom, its reverence for the function of criticism, its respect for learning and for rational exchange. They are a scholar's summary view of what the university, as we have traditionally understood it, is about. But in the surcharged atmosphere of that occasion the placating force of those sentences went unheard. Men had come to bury Caesar, not to honor Brutus; and it presently appeared, in spite of the most assiduous attention to ritual forms and outward dignities, that the essential drama of this occasion was the unpremeditated part for which there was no ready script. As Hofstadter began to speak, a group of students rose and filed counterceremonially out of the building. From that moment it was evident that whatever the speaker might say, the significance of the event could no longer be expected to lie in the spoken word, in inquiry, in civil discussion or rational exchange. The significance of the event lay

now beyond ceremony, beyond temple, even beyond the innocent ivy. It lay in the moral estrangements of men, in the
confused and terrible reality beyond the walls, which derided
this address, condemned its purposes, and accused its sincer-
ity, without a hearing.

The damage to the outward ceremony concerned no one
except in passing. What really mattered was the inner failure,
the moral failure of a society, for which there was no outward
remedy. The covenant of the intellectual community had been
in fact suspended. Hitherto that covenant had afforded a common ground, a neutral ground beyond politics or ideology,
upon which questions of public importance might be debated,
the public interest studied, and public policy formed. To inform the conduct of the public life with the resources of every
science and every art—this was the public commission of a
university in our society. But now this commission had been
vacated, there was no neutral ground, and society was without
a substitute for the agency that had once afforded it.

That, I suppose, is why I experienced such strangely
mixed emotions in meditating those invincible young, great
with the hopes of their generation, who rose in the stained
half lights of the cathedral and filed silently out of the lofty
vaulted nave in which their own commencement was being
celebrated. In the very citadel of intellectual individualism
they were daring to raise the question they had been taught to
ask. They were saying, What is the value of intellectual individualism if it leads to no community of belief and action and
reverence? We have divorced our institutions from the pursuit
of a common life and now despair that the common life has
become, even in the house of intellect, a moral desert.

My own sympathies were gravely divided. Not all were
departing. In fact, the greater number remained still seated in
their pews. Yet in spite of this I found myself reflecting that it
was not entirely clear where at that moment the university
was, whether it moved with those who were departing the
cathedral or remained behind with those who stayed. For the
question at issue—the only question that now counted—was

not men's numbers but their loyalties. Upon everyone in that great assembly, staying or leaving, lay the same demand for decision. In this breakdown of the constitution that held them together in one assembly there was no longer any room for neutrals. Each stood isolated at history's growing edge, and each was obliged to share the existential risk of shaping it.

Henry David Thoreau used to say: "Any man more right than his neighbors constitutes a majority of one." That sentence deserves to be carved in stone above the master portal of the university, so that everyone entering might know his duty. It remains of course to be determined which man is more right than his neighbors, and that determination is a matter not of pretension but of proof. The only way to prove a man's claim to be a majority of one is to show that he knows as others do not, or at least as others do not in equal measure, how to civilize their contests, how to reconcile their differences, how to teach them to be "of one mind in an house," by restoring their neutral assembly. For the neutral assembly is not what you start with; it is what you labor after. When Thoreau removed himself from Concord to the untraversed solitudes of Walden Pond, it is usually omitted to notice that he carried under his arm (besides Indian meal, a watermelon and 22 cents worth of salt pork) his Greek Homer. There is no surer revelation of the public significance of his private act. The Thoreau that went to Walden was not without company; he simply chose his company. His company was Concord's buried life—Homer and Aeschylus, Dante and Shakespeare. Our mistake is to suppose that his company was the unoffending woodchuck which, when it ravaged his beanfield, he remedially ate for dinner. Any man may be a majority of one in the wilderness of his beanfield. In that there is no problem, for if you eat the minority you need not live with it. The problem is to be a majority of one in the face of society, to show society by example where its true path lies if it would live with itself. There may be in Thoreau lessons for anchorites; but that is at all events not the social implication of his example which we Americans find redemptive and critically useful. The question raised by Thoreau is, not whether it is possible for a man to live alone, but where virtue lies, in the village or in the majority of one who labors beyond it, reading Homer and writing *Walden*, for the village's sake.

2. THE SHELTER OF THE PUBLIC ARGUMENT

The commencement address, in spite of the interruption, went on, and those sentences I have recorded commanded now my undivided practical attention. I had but one purpose, to take from this wounded institution any least trace of instruction that it might offer. All of the brute collisions of interest and selfish solicitude that were manifest in the actual rupture of the peace at Columbia were latent in our illusions of peace elsewhere. The same pattern unfolded itself beneath the thinnest residues of decency in every major institution of higher education in the land, and it concerned me to know what construction to put upon it. Therefore I attended with special care to those sentences. Spoken by a most dedicated student of human freedom, spoken with unparalleled candor on a solemn occasion, they were intended to repair the divisions of the scholarly community, to restore its ancient bond of covenant. They were, in their way, in a season that is without prophecy, prophetic. That is to say, they appealed to the unspoken traditional consent of all scholars, that the university, whatever else it is or may become, is always at last, as scholars see it, a community of inquiry. Other commissions the university may take up or put aside as society lays accidental demands upon it. But inquiry is the one commission it is forbidden to vacate if it would preserve its title for education or for service. The university can educate, it can serve, only because it commands the resources that inquiry has conferred upon it. The university is essentially, as scholars view their own company with each other, a community of inquiry—not a political faction, not an instrument of party, not a weapon of interest or privilege, but a neutral assembly of scholars gathered for the critical exchange of ideas.

Hofstadter's address was a plea for the preservation of the freedom of this neutral assembly. The neutrality of a university is the price of its freedom. Let its neutrality be doubted, all of its acts will be thought suspect, *ultra vires,* in excess of its proper authority. Let its neutrality be assured, a democratic society will license it to discuss all matters, to enter unprohibited into every avenue of rational inquiry, to pursue truth critically by demanding for every belief evidence, for every disbelief tolerance, for every decision among contending beliefs the discipline of proof, and for the right to dissent an inviolable guarantee.

These were all customary affirmations, the conventional affirmations of our society, recalled in order to restore old peace, old peace in the untranquil rubble. In any other context my consent would have been immediate and spontaneous. But in this context I recoiled, somehow gravely offended. The cause of my arrest (as I have since come to know) was Hofstadter's willingness, in his effort to preserve the freedom of the university, to isolate it, to put it beyond good and evil, beyond criticism, beyond all of the liabilities of political offense that go with public service.

What else was to be understood from that difficult proposition brought forward in defense of Columbia, that the university has no corporate views on public questions? No one who is party to the university doubts for a moment that the university is in fact capable of corporate act and policy. Its unquestionable capacity for holding corporate views on public questions is at the bottom of the universal concern to neutralize it. A modern university has all of the intricate powers for canalizing energy that belong to any chartered corporation; it is able to concentrate resources of technical skill and intelligence which sovereign states envy and which nowadays they can equal only by stealing from it. In the eye of the law the university is an artificial person, a subject of rights and duties. It can sue and be sued; it can enter into contracts with government and industry; it can employ men, borrow or beg money, own property, lease land, build skyscrapers, and sell short.

Also, if properly reminded, it can educate. Corporate views it is admitted to have on any matter that concerns it privately— for example, the question of "its own internal order," or the questions that touch upon its "basic values of freedom, rationality, inquiry, discussion." But so far as these values of free discussion and rational inquiry depend (as in some measure they always do) on public tolerances, they become inevitably public questions, and the university must necessarily hold corporate views concerning them.

In a last accounting, the education of the young of a society is the most momentous and fateful of all public questions whatever. Yet what must education be in a house divided? What must education become when tradition and old reverence fail and the generations hesitate as strangers before the covenants that once united fathers and sons? That is a public question of the first order, and about that question the university must necessarily have opinions, even when the public leaves the question temporarily or in part undecided.

Of the capacity of the university for taking sides, of its capacity for taking sides on any question public or private, there is, therefore, no room for doubt. The opinion of Hofstadter that the university takes no position on public questions must then be accounted false? No, not false. The real force of this opinion was not to describe the university but to instruct it. Not only does the university in fact take no position on public questions; it is in principle forbidden to take a position. In the language of the Carnegie Commission on Higher Education, the university has the "right and obligation not to take a position, as an institution, in electoral politics or on public issues, except on those issues which directly affect its autonomy, the freedom of its members, its financial support, and its academic functions."[2] This instruction conforms to the traditional conception of a university free of political entanglements. To perform its proper offices, the university must detach itself from the struggles of factions, sects and parties. Unimplicated spectator of history, it must put itself beyond any possible suspicion of influencing the changes it professes to

analyze. The university must enact the role of an impartial observer, set apart from all of the estranging contests that divide
us, in action or passion, in the neighborhood, the market and
the forum.

This conception of a university unimplicated in the partisanships of society was of course the very matter in contention
in that divided assembly in Saint John's. But I had not expected to hear the issue so sharply drawn; and now, hearing
it, I found myself silently repeating the line that ruined
Othello spoke in the black night of his soul, "Othello's occupation's gone!" So, it seemed to me, was the university's occupation gone, if Hofstadter's opinion of it were upheld. If the
university is systematically excluded from any part in the great
historical decisions concerning human welfare and peace and
social justice that are at wager in the public life, if it is de-
barred in its corporate capacity from interesting itself in the
public good, then I must confess that in my estimation we
have bought its freedom at too dear a price. For we have secured the freedom of the corporation at cost of denying its
public responsibility. We have denied the social obligation
that justifies our support of it, that makes its freedom important, its purpose necessary, its immunity defensible, and its
science public. Yet how shall we reconcile the university's social responsibility with the demand for neutrality that society
has laid upon it?

To perform its public office, to do its proper work, the
university must preserve itself beyond partisanship and beyond advocacy. Martin Luther—professor of theology at the
University of Wittenberg—may take a stand on public issues;
Wittenberg may not. When Luther journeys to the University
of Leipzig to meet his challenger John Eck, little Wittenberg
may from motives of local pride, in a formal disputation attended by prince and prelate and lasting eighteen days, favor
its own scholar and send Carlstadt to open the debate, Me-
lanchthon to hear it, and two hundred students armed with
battle-axes to defend it. But Wittenberg does not pretend, by
these private expressions of partiality, to bend the public ar-

gument or to influence its conclusion. The university nails no theses on church doors. Its proper work is done when it establishes the public conditions of rational exchange, when it institutes the convocation in which partisanships may be impartially heard, and collisions of opinion peaceably resolved, according to rules known and commonly admitted in advance. The university shelters the argument; therefore, in its public role, it is forbidden to be party to the argument. The university shelters the argument, but not the theses argued. Theses it leaves to partisans like Luther, on the ground that, so long as shelter is provided and actors are free to enter it, the actors will be forthcoming by their own motives, and out of their undirected exchanges an objective truth will emerge.

But we have lost sight of these large simplicities. The neutrality of the university has become in our day a profoundly ambiguous testament. We confuse neutrality with privacy, detachment with indifference, the objectivity of the impartial observer with the vacant merit of having no opinions on public questions. We have been so solicitous to preserve the freedom of the individual inquirer, to tolerate nonconformity, to license the unpopular dissent in which a new initiative may lie, that we have forgotten our equal interest in the community to which dissent is addressed, to which it must be addressed and in which it must be heard, if it is to be in any measure effective. We have forgotten, in the crowd of soliloquies, the significance of the public debate. Of that debate the university is the silent and neutral guardian. A guardian is essential, for it is the debate not the soliloquy, the public and orderly exchange of opinions where we are divided not the private holding of opinions where we are agreed, that needs protection. In an empty alley a scholar may speak the most heretical opinions with a perfect impunity. But in an empty alley, though the freedom to speak is real, in the absence of any audience there is no occasion to exercise it. The freedom of the unlistening alley is not the kind of freedom that a scholar wants or a democratic society needs. What the scholar wants, what a democracy needs, is precisely what the university affords—not silence, not unanimity, not even agreement, but the *civilization of argument*. What the university distinctively affords is the unspoken condition of all rational inquiry, a neutral ground upon which divided partisans may meet, listening as well as speaking, in order to compose their differences according to rules of evidence to which they commonly consent. Socrates used to say with disarming civility: "Let the argument lead us." That is what the neutral university says. The argument is independent of the disputants; it must be kept permanently in the public domain; and the business of keeping it there is the university's public commission.

3. "THE SUPRA-NATIONAL COMMONWEALTH OF LEARNING"

The oneness of the community of scholars is too little understood to excite public attention. It is nevertheless one of the supreme social achievements of our world, and I must ask to pause over it. If Columbia's light is eclipsed, Harvard's is exactly in that measure diminished. And the same will be true of Michigan and California, of Paris and Bologna, of Oxford and Berlin and Moscow. All are at one stroke diminished without waiting for the silly circuit of the sun. For it is after all one light, and one community that labors after it. We divide our labors and follow separate paths; but it is an illusion to suppose that because we walk beyond the sight of each other's faces our tasks are therefore private, egotistic, or insular. The scholar prepares himself in solitude; he thinks in public. The university is in fact an extended public argument, and the scholar is party to it, studies only to advance it, and deserts the role of scholar in the moment that he provincializes it.[3]

   In the beginnings of the university, in the medieval cathedral schools, to deny the public commission of the university in one place was to deny it everywhere. Such was the significance, in those early schools, of the wandering scholar, of every young Abelard "traveling through various provinces in search of discussion." The places were many; the community of inquiry was everywhere one and the same. Thus, Gerbert of Aurillac, before he became Pope Sylvester II, taught at Reims the mathematics he had learned from Arabs in Spain. Crowds of students followed Abelard wherever he moved, and followed him still, even when he sought to retire into his hermitage. John of Salisbury carried on his studies at Paris in a "pleasant exile," which his friend, the abbot of Moutier-la-Celle, distrusted as a danger to his soul.[4] All of these made visible in their migratory act the circumstance that learning makes its own center. The university is not a place or a building or a book. Take from a serious scholar his place of labor, he will find another place. Take from him the instruments of his work, he will devise other instruments. He will make the sky his shelter, and instruments of science out of base materials that lesser spirits would despise. Where, then, *is* the university? The answer is, Wherever the obligations of the community of inquiry are understood and honored in performance. There is a philosophical rightness in the fact that the earliest distinguishing mark of a university was the privilege of conferring upon scholars, when they became masters, the *ius ubique docendi,* the right to teach abroad from the place of the university.[5] The right is, literally, a right to teach *in any place whatever.* For the university is only circumstantially here or there, only accidentally at Paris or at Chartres or at Montpellier; properly and essentially, it is wherever the covenant of scholars is faithfully observed, wherever for the sake of a community of criticism men put themselves under common rules of discussion, proof, and evidence.

Consent to rules of proof and evidence is to the scholarly community what consent to law is to the political. It is the condition of covenant that underlies all civilized argument whatever. Scientists are typically blind to the social foundations of the scientific community. They look at other forms of community with a proper detachment, at their own always with an ignorant sentimentality, as if they were God's spies. They are therefore never able to grasp the social foundations of scientific objectivity. When a chemist at Columbia publishes his experiment, he addresses himself to chemists everywhere, no less to the don in Cambridge or the academician in Moscow than to the scientific faculty that works beside him in American laboratories adjacent to his own. He urges upon the world a very simple claim, a prediction that if the conditions of his experiment are reproduced, his observations will be confirmed by any candid observer. In short, proof is independent of persons. Let the chemist in Moscow reply to the American's claim, disputing it or confirming it. The consent to rule which is implied in that simple scholarly exchange has overleaped the boundaries of hemispheres and nations. Each party to the exchange views himself as meeting the other in one community of enterprise in which, whether they agree or disagree, their purposes are conjoined. They are allied as chemists in spite of the fact that they are divided as nationals. They are allied in spite even of the fact that they may circumstantially, on the matter before them, disagree. For beneath their argument, which is manifest, there subsists an agreement, which is latent and unspoken but mutual and perfectly understood. Each regards himself as party to a public conversation which anyone may enter on condition that he is willing to submit to its rules. Its rules—rules governing the admission of evidence and the meaning of proof—are the covenant of their intellectual community with each other.

Scattered among the nations of the earth, scholars are like the Jews of the dispersion. They have community by covenant, not by fact; by affirmation, not by neighborhood. They are bound to each other in one community in spite of all of the political and moral estrangements that separate them, in other connections and for other purposes, from one another. They are a nation without a territory, a people without a Zion. They never fully assemble. Their real exchanges occur in the silence of the printed word, which one writes and the other reads, and the two together join in meditating, in solitude. They are a company of absentees. Their effective community is nevertheless, in spite of their unpromising habits of hermitage and anarchy, one of the most extraordinary social inventions in history. We allude to it whenever we speak of the "scientific community" or of the "community of scholarship." But we speak, then, ambiguously. For what in fact we intend by these phrases is not the manifest university, not Columbia or Harvard or Berkeley or Moscow, but the latent community of inquiry, the latent singular community that presides in each of these but demonstrably extends beyond any one of them, the one community of affirmation beyond any campus or any nation, of which these many centers are but the local habitations and temporary seats.

The scholar is the citizen of a scientific commonwealth, of what Sir Eric Ashby has very justly described as "a supranational commonwealth of learning."[6] In the thirteenth century, when Latin was a universal language and religion a universal bond, this cosmopolitanism was outwardly visible. A student of law was able to move from Bologna to Oxford without alteration of idiom and with assurance that the same live arguments would be afoot, and the same rules of disputation honored, in the one scene as in the other. He moved very much as a modern student of law moves, speaking American, from Columbia to Berkeley, or as a modern student of physics moves, speaking mathematics, from Harvard to Moscow. But we are by inveterate habit accustomed to dignifying our separations. We believe in the places that we see more readily than in the covenants that we do not see. The modern cosmopolitan therefore appears to us to be a new kind of man, the product of the academic revolution which Christopher Jencks and David Riesman have described: "Large numbers of Ph.D.s now regard themselves almost as independent professionals like doctors or lawyers, responsible primarily to themselves and their colleagues rather than their employers, and committed to the advancement of knowledge rather than to any particular institution."[7] The players are new; the play is very old. The players enact the contemporary version of the role of the wandering scholar; they are Abelard in modern dress, distin-

guished only by the fact that each carries, with the Yankee learning in his head, a federal contract in his hand.

The regret of administrators, that the loyalty of contemporary wandering scholars is not to the university, not to Columbia or Harvard or Berkeley or Moscow, but to "the discipline," to physics or biology or political science or *belles lettres*, misses the point (as men of affairs tend always to miss it) by Zionizing it. Academic Zionism is born of a fault of understanding and a vice of imagination. All academics practice it quite shamelessly, though it must be confessed that only the sons of Harvard practice it in such measure that their vice seems splendid and imposes itself even on their betters. Politically, Zionism may be necessary; economically, it may be rewarding; intellectually, it is, like its religious analogue, a delusion of the spirit. It mistakes accident for essence, vessel for treasure, the neighborhood of the learned for the covenant that makes neighborhood count. Woodrow Wilson used to hold, with his customary elevation of mind, that Princeton was "in the nation's service," that "the school must be of the nation."[8] In the limited vision of our contemporaries the school exhausts itself—alas, poor Yorick—in Morningside Heights. But the reality of the university outreaches our poor imaginations of it. All educational statesmanship in our century will be found to lie in the perception that the latent university transcends its manifest embodiments, that the university is in fact wider than any of its political precincts, and that the nation is too narrow for it.

4. CONVOCATION OF DISSENT

Politically, amid the ideological conflicts of this century, the failure of school and nation to coincide is the university's great danger. For the university is always liable to being thought, in the life of the nation, an object of political suspicion, a source of concentrated power imperfectly amenable to ordinary political controls. The idea of an intellectual common-

wealth, of a supranational commonwealth of learning that enables men to meet beyond nationality, beyond the accidents of place or folk or parish, in one community of scholars—this idea must appear, in a world of politically divided and mutually hostile nation states, an unpardonable political offense. The accommodation of the supranational function of the university to the *de facto* political divisions of our times becomes therefore a political problem. The university is no church; it has, however, in relation to the modern state, many of the liabilities that once belonged to the church. It is too universalist to be trusted, too revolutionary to be condoned, too anarchic to be governed. Therefore it stands always in the noose of politics, poised precariously between threat of political capture and threat of political suspension.

In spite of this melancholy predicament, the university has exercised itself to know everything except its own relation to society. In times of social or political crisis, it is of all agencies of society the agency least informed concerning the duties that can properly be required of it, or that it must properly require of itself. Let me cite a modern instance.

In October 1969 the faculty of Princeton University refused by an overwhelming majority (147 to 7) to take a corporate stand on the Vietnam war.

In May 1970, outraged by the announcement that United States troops had been ordered into Cambodia and that aerial bombing of North Vietnam had been resumed, the same faculty reversed itself and by a vote of 261 to 12, 36 voices abstaining, denounced the act of the government.

We must not allow ourselves to suppose that these contrary resolutions were the acts of ignorant or careless or capricious men. They were, on the contrary, the passionately debated acts of an assembly of concerned scholars, driven by events to reflect upon the responsibilities of their own community. Their vacillation is as tragic and terrible as it is typical of a whole generation of scholars. Intellectually, scholars command all of the inherited wisdom of the race; morally, they live, as the least of us are condemned to live, *ex tempore*, in

revolution's transient establishments. Their learning does not extricate them from their historical predicament; it causes them, however, to experience the conflicts of their inherited roles with an unparalleled poignancy. Every scholar struggles with the citizen in himself, and none entirely succeeds in putting off the question the citizen raises, whether the obligation of the scholar is compatible with the responsibility of the man. We are Antigone without heaven. The conflicts of our institutions confuse our loyalties, and all men halt, even the most thoughtful and punctiliously informed and morally scrupulous among them halt, uncertain of their duties, not because they wear their duties lightly, but because the duties themselves are inconsistent, one duty requires what the other forbids, and in nature's trembling silence there appears to be no way of deciding which duty must prevail.

We ask, Was Princeton's refusal to take a position in October a duty or an aberration? Was its political condemnation of the government in the following May a precedent or a blunder? We are vexed by our dumb inability to say. The opinion spoken on the occasion was no doubt formally correct: the faculty is without legal authority to bind the university; only the board of trustees is competent to act in the person of the corporation. But that holding, though formally true, is historically trivial. For the problem before us is not what the university is to *do* but what the university is to *be*. These questions bring us face to face with constitutional issues, with issues that touch the fundamental charter and idea of the university in our society. The constitution of the university is an unfinished business, and to finish it we need above all what our history fails to afford, a conception of the positive role of a neutral in the public life.

By the *neutrality* of the university I understand the obligatory refusal of the corporation to identify itself with any of the partisan positions that are contested in theory within it or that are agitated in fact beyond it. But I intend also, besides this bare obligation of detachment, a positive commission. The positive exercise of neutrality in the university is what

ordinarily we entitle the *function of criticism*. In the commonwealth of learning there is no room for dogma; every claim to
truth stands permanently exposed to the full range of objec-
tions that the most acute, the best informed and most determined skeptics may choose to bring against it. For what really
we mean in calling truths scientific is not that any attempt to
prove them has perfectly succeeded but that every attempt to
disprove them has demonstrably failed; they have survived
the attritions of doubt that a neutral community of inquiry, in
its ordinary process, turns upon them. Scholars are as partisan
a breed as any other, and if truth were available only to inquirers who came seeking it without passion or predilection,
we should have none to ponder or to mend. What is essential
to the neutrality of the university is not the elimination of partisanship in scholars but the systematic use of it, the systematic use of conflict of opinion in order to realize, from oppositions of argument, one truth. The university is in principle
a self-correcting system, which enables us to do together what
we could not do apart. Its proper analogue is a parliament. It
performs in society the peculiar and indispensable function
which I may perhaps best describe as *the systematic convocation of dissent*.

A political parliament and a university differ in very important respects from each other. They are, however, in this
alike, that within each of them all manner of competing interests and prejudices and raw partisanships are gathered. Individuals frankly opposed in the broad society are in each of
these convocations brought together. They are brought together, not by kinship or neighborhood, not by stupor of instinct or similarity of temperament, but by community of undertaking. And in each case the community exacts from all
who would be party to it a consent to rules of order which
enable them, in spite of their oppositions, to act together.

Every time the Congress of the United States acts upon a
substantive motion, it declares its view on a public question.
It is the business of a political parliament to generate such
views, to generate them in spite of the internal divisions

among its members, and to confer upon them by the due process of debate a corporate status, a claim upon general consent that they did not have before convocation and could not have without it. A parliamentary body begets out of collisions of private interests a public policy that is capable of obliging conduct even in the parties whose interests it has, in a given instance, disallowed.

Now a university behaves on occasion exactly according to that pattern. In the formal meetings of its faculty, in senate and academic council, it frames general policy for its own community. Scholars make a fashion of pretending that such general matters are beneath their notice. In this they indulge a dangerous delusion. The housekeeping details of self-government, which seem so tedious and trivial when they are done, would be thought to shake the earth if they were left undone. Yet still, in their essential instinct for what is central and primary in the university, scholars are unerringly right in their judgment that a meeting of the faculty is the last of all places to go seeking truth. In all of its primary work the university is obliged to forgo direct resolutions by majority. For its business is not to conclude argument but on the contrary to institute it, to institute the process of argument in such neutral terms that the parties to the argument will consent, careless of majorities, to be bound by it. Therefore, if you would deal with the primary questions of the university, not with its incidents of housekeeping but with the great critical questions that preoccupy the best intellects, you must return from the general assembly to the study and the laboratory, the lecture, and the seminar, to the informal and uncalculated exchanges of solitaries in shirtsleeves who meet each other in the hall and, forgetful of what they had set out to do, stand endlessly talking till the janitor restores good sense, sends them home, and turns out the lights.

I recall my reflection on first reading of Princeton's denunciation of the policy of the United States government in Cambodia. A private college in New Jersey was presuming to condemn the action of the most powerful government in all the world. My thought was that the interest of this act was not in what Princeton now did but in what it now disqualified itself from doing. The faculty of a great institution of learning had in a heat exchanged its public commission for a private gesture. I was no less disturbed that this move was taken by honorable and decent men who acted out of a horror of war that I fully shared. With their sense of outrage I was in complete sympathy. Their prudence I forbade myself to judge. The university had, in a partisan act, condemned the government. Whether it was wise in doing so, whether this act was warranted or in fact quite safe in an institution that could not carry on its researches without the support of the government—this question could without impertinence be raised and no doubt troubled the reflections of a sorely tried administration.[9] But that risk was at all events one the faculty was content to run, and I was by no means in a position, now after the fact, to judge of it, even had I been disposed to do so. Yet still it seemed to me that everything that really mattered to them and to me was compromised by their resolution. For the real question was not a question of prudence; it was a question of principle. If the university allows its intellectual authority to be measured against political power, it compromises its claim to an authority that is independent of political power. The intellectual authority of the community of scholars is incontestable; its political power—the political power that belongs to the community of scholars as a corporation—is perfectly negligible. If we confuse the university's authority with its power, we shall not make its power incontestable; we shall make its authority negligible.

The account I read labored over the question whether the faculty of Princeton was entitled to speak for the university—for trustees and administration, students and alumni—as well as for itself. I was content to relinquish that question to the inconsequent mercies of the lawyers. It was enough for my purposes that the faculty spoke for the faculty. But the question arose, now that it had spoken, What importance should

be attached to its resolution? What special claim had this resolution on my acceptance which was not had also, and had
with an equal political authority, by the resolution of an assembly of greengrocers? And I was obliged to answer, though
this was one of the most extraordinary learned assemblies in
the world, that it had none.

5. THE POLITICAL PATH OF THE UNIVERSITY

The convocation of dissent is in our day a very little understood art, and the practice of it under the conditions of modern life frequently baffles us. Of this only are we perfectly assured, that in the new relation of science and society there can
be no such thing as a university beyond politics. A mere silence on public questions will not prove the detachment of the
university; facelessness will not prove its innocence; quaran-
tine will not prove its loyalty. The path of a university is un-
avoidably a political path for the reason that neutrality is un-
avoidably a political role. The problem of a neutral is not how
to be out of the world but how to be in it—how to be in it
without being of it.

Plato's Academy was a deliberated seclusion from society.
The modern university has become, not by necessity but by
historical drift, an undeliberated exposure to it. The drift, the
designlessness, needs remedy. Yet if I am asked in which of
these contexts—seclusion or exposure—the work of objective
criticism is in the long run more likely to prosper, I reply un-
hesitatingly in favor of the latter. It is an error to suppose that
the neutrality of the university is advanced or secured by iso-
lating it from the political stresses of the public life. Neutrality
implies, in the party who undertakes it, a self-imposed duty,
an obligation of detachment, with respect to matters about
which others are politically divided. Neutrality signifies, in
short, a political posture, not a political omission. That is why
the effort to isolate the university from political strains is always bound to fail. Isolationism is as bankrupt a policy in the

university as in the nation. It rests on the same delusion. In the life of nations it confuses peace with the absence of war; in the life of universities neutrality with the absence of views on public questions.

Politically, for a university in the American scene, to strike the balance of a neutral is a very delicate problem of statesmanship. Every age in America has its Alien and Sedition Acts, its Know-Nothing hangups, its vigilantes, Klans and McCarthyisms, its John Birch societies, the recurrent eruptions of hate and suspicion in which, under color of defending the free pattern of our life, we betray it. Such rough oppositions are a permanent presence in our troubled history, and any authentic understanding of the path of our society must recognize this paradox of the American character. We banish the Inquisition; we harbor the Inquisitor. The Inquisitor is one of the uneliminable risks of our special brand of freedom. There is, after all, nothing in the conception of an open society that forbids scoundrels to enter it, or entering it to be heard, or being heard even for a time (if only for a time) to carry the day. The American holds that if you find no scoundrel in an open society, you may doubt its openness. And in this he is probably right, though he is perhaps mistaken in concluding that the scoundrel deserves therefore his affection, his emoluments, and a seat in his Senate. At all events, the virtue of the university in America must not be made to depend on its being populated by Sunday saints and men perfect in goodwill. Its virtue comes from the capacity of its process to civilize the disputes of ordinary unregenerate egotists and scoundrels like you and me.

In 1917, when the United States entered the war in Europe, the neutrality of the university was our immediate first casualty. The free public exchange of opinion on which the life of the university is grounded was in danger of suspension on all campuses, and stood in fact suspended on most. The call that went out in those days was not to politicize the university but on the contrary to depoliticize it. There was said to be a difference. Then as now, however, the object was the same, to silence the dissident voices which some dared to raise. Nicholas Murray Butler, the redoubtable president of Columbia, left no doubt where, in the hour of trial, his university stood. "What had been tolerated before becomes intolerable now. What had been wrongheadedness was now sedition. What had been folly was now treason." The university stood with the nation, and President Butler encouraged the nation to take comfort from the fact that he was there too, the bearer (lest anyone suppose the university to have no corporate opinions on public questions) of "the University's last and only warning to any among us, if such there be, who are not with whole heart and mind and strength committed to fight with us to make the world safe for democracy." [10]

That is the representative voice of a generation, and the generation heard it with a glad noise. Its effect upon the university was instant and calamitous; it drove criticism elsewhere. Charles A. Beard, having resigned his place in the university, wrote on independently, performing still the public offices of a scholar from a farm chair in Connecticut. The only effect of the warning was to divorce dissent from the convocation in which dissent is socially productive and scientifically most useful. The warning produced not the neutrality of a university but only the semblance of it, the outward discreet illusion of consent that lies over the university wherever its members are obliged to remain silent on questions of public importance because the corporation has taken a stand.

A. Lawrence Lowell, the president of Harvard University, was unwilling to settle for so negative a result. With the unsentimental toughness of a lawyer and student of government, he perceived that if the university allows itself to restrain the pronouncements of its professors in any instance, the public will conclude that there is no distinction to be drawn between the voice of the university and the voice of the professor.

If the university or college censors what its professors may say, if it restrains them from uttering something that it does not approve, it thereby assumes responsibility for that which it permits them to say. This . . . is a responsibility which an institution of learning would be very unwise in assuming.

. . . There is no middle ground. Either the university assumes full responsibility for permitting its professors to express certain opinions in public, or it assumes no responsibility whatever, and leaves them to be dealt with like other citizens by the public authorities according to the law of the land.[11]

That is a hard saying; but it is, I think, true. Academic freedom has not been designed to serve the private interests of academics; its proper object is to serve the public interests of society.[12] The university is not (as a later day will express it) "a sanctuary from the general law." If the law of the land will not protect the right of dissent in the citizen, the university is quite powerless to protect it in the professor. The university is, however, by delegation of the law itself, a sanctuary for the public argument that it shelters. The neutral convocation of dissent is a public office, the most powerful agency that human beings have invented for realizing, in matters of belief, the principled infinality of an open society. In the right conduct of a university any opinion of a professor may be heard without impediment. But the motive of the university in permitting the opinion to be spoken is not the professor's right to speak it but the society's need to hear it.

In a journal entry made during the abolition controversy, Ralph Waldo Emerson, secluded in his study, once asked himself by what right in such times, in times when the world's rude anvil was being struck, he should be sheltered from the noise of the day's impassioned alarms. What man has the right of seclusion or soliloquy when the people's counsels are divided and society stands perilously on the brink of a civil war?

His answer was: No man. No man has a right of seclusion. But some have the *duty* of it. Shall we, commissioned to perform the tasks of critical reflection in society, desert our posts and, in order to do what another may do equally and as well, leave tragically undone the duty entrusted to our care?

Emerson remained in his study. But he had perceived what we have forgotten and what those who have sought to politicize the university have in fact meant to say, that the work of thought is public business, and the shelter of argument a public trust.

NOTES

1. *New York Times,* June 5, 1968, p. 34, cols. 3–6. The address is printed in full, under the title "The 214th Columbia University Commencement Address," in 37 *The American Scholar* (Autumn 1968): 583–589.

2. *A Digest of Reports and Recommendations, December 1968–October 1971,* Carnegie Commission on Higher Education (Berkeley, 1971), "Dissent and Disruption: Proposals for Consideration by the Campus (June 1971)," p. 78.

3. If you have an eye for such things, you may see that ancient character of the university outwardly preserved in the public oral examination of a doctor of philosophy. The oral defense of the dissertation is the poor remnant in our midst of the medieval *disputatio.* The thesis is the private business of the candidate; but the disputation, the argument that confirms or disconfirms the thesis, is the public business of the university. A man becomes a master by qualifying himself for the conduct of the public business; there is no other mastery. But these once eloquent old forms are nowadays for the most part lost on us. Their meaning is unremembered, and in our scattered citadels of intellectual individualism we are without forms to declare decently to the world what we all believe but have forgotten how to celebrate, that scholarship is a public office.

4. Helene Wieruszowski, *The Medieval University: Masters, Students, Learning* (Princeton, N.J.: Van Nostrand, 1966), pp. 122–123, 130–132, 136.

5. Hastings Rashdall, *The Universities of Europe in the Middle Ages,* edited by F. M. Powicke and A. B. Emden (Oxford: Clarendon Press, 1895 [1936]), vol. I, pp. 10–19. "The Universities in their earliest days," says Rashdall, "had no buildings of their own, and the fact is one which is of primary importance for the appreciation of the genius and history of the institution. Their power depended wholly upon the facility with which they could move from town to town: and when a University or a large section of it had decamped from the place, there were no effects left behind for the authorities to attach" (I, 189). Not until the fifteenth century did the universities begin to acquire buildings of their own (I, 219).

6. Eric Ashby, *Technology and the Academics, An Essay on Uni-*

versities and the Scientific Revolution (New York: St. Martin's Press, 1958 [1962]), pp. 43–46. Cf. John F. A. Taylor, *The Masks of Society, An Inquiry into the Covenants of Civilization* (New York: Appleton-Century-Crofts, 1966), pp. 156–172, 222–238.

7. Christopher Jencks and David Riesman, *The Academic Revolution* (Garden City, N.Y.: Doubleday, 1968), p. 14. Cf. Carl Kaysen, *The Higher Learning, the Universities and the Public: The Stafford Little Lectures at Princeton University, 1968* (Princeton, N.J.: Princeton University Press, 1969), pp. 15–16.

8. "Princeton in the Nation's Service," 22 *Forum* (December 1896): 465–466.

9. Sir Eric Ashby has written: "The universities in Holland, Western Germany, France and the British Commonwealth, and all but a few private universities in America, now depend on the state for finance. If the state withdrew its patronage most of them could not survive six months." 1 *Minerva, A Review of Science, Learning and Policy* 21 (Autumn, 1962).

10. Richard Hofstadter and Wilson Smith, editors, *American Higher Education, A Documentary History* (Chicago: University of Chicago Press, 1961), vol. II, pp. 843–844. The quotation is drawn from President Butler's Commencement Day Address, June 6, 1917, in Columbia University Archives.

11. A. Lawrence Lowell, *At War with Academic Traditions in America* (Cambridge, Mass.: Harvard University Press, 1934), p. 271. Cf. Judge Charles E. Wyzanski, Jr., "Sentinels and Stewards," *Harvard Alumni Bulletin* (January 23, 1954), p. 316:

"A University is the historical consequence of the medieval *studium generale*—a self-generated guild of students or of masters accepting as grounds for entrance and dismissal only criteria relevant to the performance of scholarly duties. The men who become full members of the faculty are not in substance our employees. They are not our agents. They are not our representatives. They are a fellowship of independent scholars answerable to us only for academic integrity.

"We undertake the responsibility of handling infractions of university codes occurring within the times and places where our certificate operates. On these matters we possess the best available evidence, we have familiar canons to apply, and we have established processes of judgment and punishment.

"What faculty members do outside their posts, we should leave to outside authority."

12. Cf. the American Association of University Professors' *1940 Statement of Principles on Academic Freedom and Tenure:* "Institutions

of higher education are conducted for the common good and not to further the interest of either the individual teacher or the institution as a whole." Clark Byse and Louis Joughin have written: "Academic freedom and tenure do not exist because of a particular solicitude for the human beings who staff our academic institutions. They exist, instead, in order that society may have the benefit of honest judgment and independent criticism which otherwise might be withheld because of fear of offending a dominant social group or transient social attitude." *Tenure in American Higher Education: Plans, Practices, and the Law* (Ithaca, N.Y.: Cornell University Press, 1959), p. 4. See also Fritz Machlup, "On Some Misconceptions Concerning Academic Freedom," in 41 *AAUP Bulletin* (Winter 1955): 753–784: "For, it is in the interest of society at large, not just in the interest of the professors, that academic freedom is defended. . . . Ultimately, academic freedom is a right of the people."

2

THE PUBLIC
COMMISSION
OF THE UNIVERSITY

1. INDUSTRIAL REVOLUTION

When Abraham Lincoln set his signature to the Morrill Act of 1862, he can hardly have suspected that the instrument which he thus fixed into law was as radical a charter of new freedom as the Proclamation of Emancipation. The Proclamation belongs to the same year; it is known to all the world as a prophetic shaking of the foundations of the nation. To the majority of Americans the Morrill Act is known not at all, and even those who know it have failed to see in it the germ of a new order of intellect in human affairs.[1] Yet there is no single piece of legislation in American intellectual history whose principle has been so inexhaustibly transforming, or whose benefits have been so profuse and permanent, in the nation's peace.

The Morrill Land Grant Act was the charter of America's quietest revolution. The act provided that 17,430,000 acres of the public domain—30,000 acres per Senator and Congressman in each state—were to be set aside for the endowment of colleges of agriculture and the mechanical arts. If the gentleman scholars of the old academy sniffed at this prospect of cattle stalls and coke ovens in the neighborhood, they behaved according to the predictable pattern of every dying aristocracy. A dying aristocracy will always suppose dignity to lie in titles, history in heraldry, and privilege in a capacity for splendid irrelevance. But the plain men who were the intended beneficiaries of the Morrill Act, "seven-eights of the race," were disposed neither to cultivate this illusion nor to honor it. "Books," Emerson had written, "are for the scholar's idle times." They had not read Emerson for nothing, and if the cattle stall and the coke oven were an imperfect interpretation of that dark saying, they were at all events nearer to Emerson's meaning than the learned scholars whom he offended.

The thing to be attended to in the land-grant institutions was not the establishment, which was modest enough, but the principle behind the establishment, which was without precedent or historical parallel. The principle was implicit in the announced purpose of the law, "to promote the liberal and practical education of the industrial classes in the several pursuits and professions in life." Frankly and unashamedly, the land-grant charter held that there is no part of human life that is beneath the notice of the university; that there is no positive labor of society that has not its proper dignity. But it held also, beyond this, that thought and action are indivorcible, that the place of the academy is in the world not beyond it, that it is part of the business of the university to demonstrate the connection of knowledge, art, and practice. "The moral conditions being equal," Francis Wayland had written in 1850, "the progress of a nation in wealth, happiness, and refinement, is measured by the universality of its knowledge of the laws of nature, and its skill in adapting these laws to the purposes of man."[2] The Morrill Act was conceived in the spirit of that announcement. In principle, it required that the dignity of every enterprise, including the enterprise of the university, be expressible in terms of the values it releases in human life, and if such value cannot be shown, then it held the dignity to be vacant, and its claim, however sanctified by custom, to be null and void.

It is very difficult in our century to grasp the radical novelty of this charter as it was understood by those who proposed it. That is perhaps the best measure of the thoroughness of its conquest in our society. There are American universities, now as then, that are not land-grant institutions. But there is no university in the land, or for that matter anywhere in the world, which has not been obliged to accommodate itself to the principle of the Morrill Act.

In 1862 the significance of an education suited to the needs of an industrial society could be lost on no one. The establishment of the land-grant institutions was an incontestable breach in the social barrier that separated the higher learning—the learning of the clergyman, the lawyer, the physician, and the gentleman scholar—from the common life. The letters patent that had immemorially authorized a monopoly of knowledge in the learned professions were in one stroke rescinded. The Morill Act was a declaration of the dignity of the common life, of the life discovered in the ordinary episodes of productive industry and health and ordered peace, of the uncloseted life of the farmer, the mechanic and the tradesman, whose crop was their weathered memorial, whose railroad was their sufficient monument, whose market was the unlettered concourse of their generations.

In the season of the Reformation, Erasmus said of himself: "I have sought to be a spectator of this tragedy." He is the type figure of the humanist in modern times—urbane, learned, judicious, aware of all of the fierce partisan alternatives of his day, satisfied with none of them, too fastidious to be wholly committed to any of them. Intellectually, Erasmus understood the forces at work in his world better than any man of his generation; morally, he was an absentee. He failed, of course. The times swept past him as they have swept past the academic humanist in every season of the world's birth. For the right of the secluded intellect is not to be achieved by spectators; neither can it be preserved by them. The secluded intellect depends upon the social immunities that permit it, and there are seasons of moral arrest in human history in which no man is privileged to walk apart, as Erasmus aspired to walk, unbruised by the grit of the earth.

An old academy might affect to work under the eye of eternity; the new academy was to work under the eye of time, in history's solemn pulse, subject to all of the real and present stresses that divide men and nations in their encounter with each other.

The nation at war, placed in the open lap of a continent, free to expand upon a physical frontier that was its unchallenged preserve, was destined to become the major path of the Industrial Revolution. In 1862, the great wind of the modern transformation brooded already over the face of the land. Powerful, irresistible, ambiguous, as inventive in war as in peace, it gathered increase as it moved; and it moved wherever men walked, so that at last men walked after it, led by it, deserting the somnolent villages, vacating old economies and all of their most ancient estates and conditions of life, in an astonished vision of new wealth. The Industrial Revolution had discovered the Vertical Frontier—not the waste deserts of outer space, but the uncharted domain that a technical transformation of the modes of production laid open, a strange untrafficked territory, illimitable and untouched, that would in one century empty the countryside and populate the cities and create, in the place of the agrarian society that Jefferson knew, the urban society that we know.[3] In our day 84 percent of the population is congregated in cities on one tenth of the land, and from the cities comes 90 percent of the gross national product. The problem, as some men perceived, was not how to resist this wind of increase, but how to use it, how to turn increase into new freedom, power into commonwealth, and factory into grace.

But this problem of the Vertical Frontier had still to be demonstrated and was left for our century to ponder obscurely. The Industrial Revolution was the work, not of statesmen or social reformers, but of artisans, of plain men of the shop and forge, shrewd tinkerers whose intelligence was superior to their occupations, whose science was humble in their hands. Their proficient imagination was exercised only where use required it. If the consequence of reforming a craft was to transform a society, that consequence was at all events not their intention. Their intention was simply to increase production, to increase the production of society if that public advantage should chance to follow, but in any case to increase the production of the man or the firm if it should not.

They had made, however, a discovery. Essentially they had discovered in the tool in the hand of the craftsman the secret of all increase of power in our commerce with nature. If I dig with my hands in the crust of the earth, my hands will bleed. If between my hand and the soil I interpose a shell or a spade, then out of the labor of my body the crust is broken and my hand remains whole. But this device may be indefinitely repeated. Let a machine be interposed between the man and the spade. The spade cuts, the machine labors, the hole is dug. The man is absolved to turn his attentions to other labors, and at last to turn his attentions to the only question that really concerns him, what manner of life he shall frame for himself in relation to his neighbor who also digs. That is the essential genius, it is also the presiding liability, of the Industrial Revolution wherever it occurs. Its pattern is always the same. Always between the man and that part of the environment at which he directly labors a tool is interposed, and the man is freed from his bondage to nature, set at liberty to perform his proper tasks, exactly in the measure that these interpositions are multiplied.

In the twentieth century the liberty to perform the tasks proper to ourselves has become, it must be admitted, an acute embarrassment. Freedom from the bondage to nature has been discovered to be the most dangerous revelation of our human condition. It has exposed, as no premonitory preachment could have done, the strangest paradox of all economic sufficiency, that Adam fed is a greater problem to himself than Adam unfed. Unfed, Adam's life has meaning in the labor to which he is committed; fed, his life can have meaning only in the labor to which he commits himself. Take from a twentieth-century laborer his servitude to the tasks of subsistence, you have no longer a man but only a bewildered animal with nothing to do and only vacuity to celebrate. His freedom is without commission, since he has prepared no commission for himself, and society prepares none for him. We are a race without sacraments. Our baffled concern with the uses of leisure has caused us to regret the freedom that has conferred it. And in this aimless absolution and disgust our former condition of servitude must appear to us a lost paradise that only poverty, merciful poverty, can restore. It is easier to dig postholes, even with bloody hands, than to confront the stark moral problem which the Industrial Revolution has placed, without proclamation of government or intimation of deity, out of the hands of simple artisans, in our path.

But in 1862, by grace of poverty, men found absolution in the postholes that still needing digging, and the first commission of the land-grant institutions was to assist in that remarkable, if temporary, office.

It has become evident that there have been in fact two Industrial Revolutions. The first revolution was the work of the hand; the second is the work of the head. In the first revolution, invention depended on the fortuitous conjunction of the man with the task. During World War I, when Thomas Edison was employed by the Navy Department, he requested that an assistant be assigned to his shop "to do the numbers." That simple memorandum is the sufficient emblem of a season. Edison's unquestionable gift was a gift not of general science but of specific artifice; his performance was the product not of method but of relevant ingenuity and patient tact. It was so with the great majority of his predecessors. Their science was as limited as their experience was unborrowed, and if their capacity for observation was majestic, it was as singularly immune to transfer as the art of Rembrandt.

The second Industrial Revolution, which is the scientifically directed revolution we now know, traverses, if not always so imaginative a path, at all events a less lonely one.[4] It is the path originally set for the land-grant institutions. The land-grant institutions were designed to systematize the work of intelligence, to bring method to bear on the tasks of experiment, to put general science at the service of the hand and the hand at the service of common humanity. If it is true (as an early enthusiast claimed) that a peck of gypsum added to an acre will return an increase of a ton of clover hay, is it not fitting that a farmer should know that, or that a soils chemist should instruct him to it? And shall a people that has a frontier for its threshold and a continent for its storeroom hesitate at the illimitable prospect of an industrial civilization, informed by science, that shall banish ignorance with other poverty?

There are of course rejoinders to be made. But in 1862 very few were prepared to make them, and of those who were prepared none was in a position to make himself heard. Who shall argue with a ton of clover hay? The utility of science was a demonstrable fact of the world. Who commands knowledge commands nature, and commanding nature may command also men. The uses of that power to command men set indeed another problem. But it was assumed that this problem was as amenable to the direction of the sciences as any other and that in a nation exploding with industrial energies and initiatives it was at all events essential, competitively, to garner the power first while the getting was good.

So men garnered and got. They razed the timber from the mountainsides with an efficient art informed by science, leaving stumps and erosions where formerly the forests grew, and floods in the valleys where a peck of gypsum added to an acre once returned a ton of clover hay. They mined the soil, careless that a peck of gypsum stolen from an acre will diminish its product and, if the theft is long repeated, will at last produce a dustbowl where no clover will grow at all. They flocked to the cities and dwelt huddled in suburbs and ghettos, sky-scrapers and slum tenements. Their factories poured forth all of the commodities of splendid opulence in peace and war. Their market was peopled by corporations and labor unions. They discovered the possibilities of combination, that it is possible to channel and concentrate the power of men as it is possible to channel and concentrate the power of other parcels of nature; that pooled wealth and passive ownership can un-dertake risks which no individual would hazard; that if men may be persuaded for a working wage to divest themselves of the right to direct their own labors, and a giant undertaking be so divided that each laborer performs an assigned mechan-ical part of it, trivial in itself but consequent in orchestration, their concert may accomplish what no one of them could ac-complish alone and what the aggregate of all of them together could not accomplish if they worked separately. The wealth of their society was vastly increased, but the contrasts between wealth and poverty were greater than they ever were. The di-vision between the rich and the poor remained, not because the society did not produce utility enough to satisfy all needs, but because society was powerless to distribute utility accord-ing to need. The aggravation of the social problem which was the result of the Industrial Revolution was, like the revolution itself, intended by no one. But there was no party to the soci-ety who did not experience its effects, and there were some—the immigrant, the black, the dusty dispossessed, the mute forgotten poor—for whom its effects were calamitous and des-ecrating.

One would suppose that from the ministrations of the quiet sciences there could result only a lucid peace. But lucid peace is precisely what we do not have and what, as we have begun to see, the study of techniques of production will not afford. Even the applications of the social sciences, in schools heretofore unheard of—schools of police administration and public management, schools of marketing and communications, schools of urban design and international affairs—have failed to afford it. We have neighborhood but no covenant, wealth but no commonwealth, privacy but no republic.

Where shall a remedy be sought? Shall we seek it in the tragic reflections of historians and philosophers and poets, in a resurrection of the *studia humaniora* of Erasmus, in what used to be called the tradition of the liberal arts? I have been educated in that tradition and would be nothing without it. Yet I am obliged to say, in candor, that I no longer trust this answer. I no longer trust it, not because it is misleading or deceptive, but because, in the present degradation of the humanist tradition, it is no longer in fact an answer. A return to the rituals of appreciation in the humanities is not a solution to the ills of an industrial civilization; it is but a restatement of the problem. And if we allow ourselves to rest with our inheritance, treating what was once the education of a free mind as an indolent absolution from the tasks of our society, we betray it. We empty it of all but its ornamental value. Gentility without price, it becomes what one of the great spirits of my generation was wont to call "cheap grace."

No, the remedy of the moral arrest of an industrial society must be sought in a renewal of criticism, in the exercise of the free intellect, turned upon the actualities of the market, the university, and the forum, that is, upon the objective institutional conditions under which our human community is realized.

That there are material conditions of human society no one doubts, and the great, if imperfectly envisaged, success of the Morrill Act lay in the willingness of plain men to take these conditions seriously. But that there are, besides these material conditions of human society, formal conditions as well, conditions of civility, the instituted restraints that men lay upon themselves and consent to honor in their acts, in order that they might have society at all—this fell beyond the contemplation of the writers of the Morrill Act. They were practical men of the world, and in pursuit of their purposes they took simply for granted the social foundations of their intercourse with each other. They took them for granted exactly as the speakers of a language take for granted the conventions of syntax that are implicit in their community of discourse, or as practicing scientists take for granted the rules of proof and evidence that are essential to their community of inquiry, or as the buyers and sellers in a market take for granted the unspoken rules of the market that govern their peaceful interchanges. Such rules of consent, though they are nowhere noticed or even alluded to until they have been violated or abridged, appear in every domain of civilized activity. They are not matters of sentiment; they are the unexposed foundations of moral consent upon which our communities, such fragmentary communities as we have, are reared.

For example, let the problem be, to understand the formal conditions of the peace of the market. The market is not the City of God. Yet it may without impertinence be asked, What rules are indispensably necessary if marketers are to frame, in spite of their competitions and divisions, normal expectations of each other? In this enterprise, if we are serious about it, we are forbidden to treat theft as the norm. The market is a community of exchange. The thief in the marketplace is party to the neighborhood but not party to the community; the marketer in the marketplace is party to both. What are his assumptions? What articles of tacit civility must he subscribe to, if he is in fact to enter upon that remarkable estate of marketer?

Every marketer must be able to assume, as falling within the general consent of all parties to the market, at least two rules: first, a rule of reciprocal exchange, that for something given something shall be had in return; second, a rule of voluntary bargain, that no exchange, no transfer of rights, shall be accounted binding into which the parties to the exchange have not voluntarily entered. These rules will not prevent marketers from going broke. They nevertheless admit rights to lie in persons, and persons to be gathered under terms of peace in one society. They are the tacit but indefeasible conditions of any market, without which there could be no market at all.

Without them theft would be sufficient and exchange superfluous. They are the unwritten constitution—what I describe as
the *covenant* [5]—of the economic community.

That there are such formal conditions of human community, conditions of peace accessible to understanding and amenable to positive construction, no man who has watched the
deprivations of dignity in twentieth-century wars and Nazi
concentration camps and American urban slums can any
longer question. Many patterns of society are consistent with
the human dignity. Some, however, demonstrably prohibit it
and abort its essential conditions. And to know those conditions, to know in every domain of civilized life the formal conditions without which the dignity of persons is not preserv-
able in any measure, is in fact the study of all positive peace
among men.

The duty that lies upon us is not to rescind the principle
of the Morrill Act but, on the contrary, to extend it, to extend
it to the foundations of our public life.

"The moral conditions being equal, the progress of a nation in wealth, happiness, and refinement, is measured by the
universality of its knowledge of the laws of nature, and its skill
in adapting these laws to the purposes of man."

We have acted in the spirit of that announcement; but we
have neglected in embracing the progress of the nation, Wayland's provision, that the moral conditions must be equal.

2. THE PATTERN OF THE GUILD

My neighbor across the street is a carpenter. He views my
helplessness in matters of manifest construction with an in-
dulgent and most tolerant sympathy. Therefore, in all mechanical enterprises I am his unbonded apprentice and obedient
employer. In all of the emergencies of domestic economy I
summon him, and he comes always with a dependable quiet
patience, like the god out of the derrick in the Greek drama,
bringing bandages to me and merciful remedies to my arrested
household.

We have known each other these twenty years, and my neighbor is now so confident that I have no future in the builder's trade that he does not hesitate to share with me its last secrets. Once when we were working together he showed me how to plot a right angle on a surface. A carpenter simply lays out a triangle the sides of which have the proportions 3-4-5: the angle described by the two shorter sides is a right angle. I asked him why. He said: "John, it don't matter *why*. Just do it!" So I did it. And he was, as always in these matters, exasperatingly right.

Perhaps I should not have asked him while he was holding aloft the other end of a timber. But I confess that I was carried away by my satisfaction with this rule of thumb he had chosen to share with me. The simple rule he gave me was older than he knew or even began to surmise. It was old beyond any carpenter's imagination, older than the Pythagorean theorem, older than geometry itself. When learned historians repeat to one another that the origins of geometry are to be found among the land surveyors in ancient Egypt, they dignify as truth a piece of learned foolishness. All that they properly mean is that the surveyors in Egypt, in restoring the boundaries erased annually by the inundations of the Nile, employed my neighbor's rule of 3-4-5. For more than four thousand years the formula has been repeated, without loss of utility or increase of light, in the unbroken oral tradition that links Egypt to my carpenter. This rough, uncelebrated tradition by which the crafts are handed down is distinct in principle from the geometry of the mathematicians. Ignorant of Euclid, careless of Pythagoras, it has the impolite kind of life that belongs to kitchen recipes, and it would link Egypt to my carpenter even if Euclid had never thought. If it is indeed true, as the poet says, that "Euclid alone has looked on Beauty bare," I assure the world that my carpenter, who is a Methodist and a Republican, is quite incapable of any such indecency. What interests my carpenter is the formula, not the derivation; the increase of power, not the progress of the understanding. And I suspect, if one were to have asked an

Egyptian land surveyor why his rule worked, he would have replied, then as now, with my carpenter's brief patience: "John, it don't matter *why*. Just do it!"

This pattern of social transmission has been in fact, historically, the education of mankind. All men depend upon it in some measure. For most of us it is the only education we ever know. The whole of our social inheritance is the summary conclusion of an unremembered argument. The conclusion is known; it is used; its justification is presumed to lie in its manifest utility, in its incontestable efficiency as routine, as formula, as recipe, for preserving old treasure. What further demonstration can be wanted or reasonably required? Why should the inheriting generations labor superfluously, repeating old costs, taxing themselves to rediscover what the fathers have already sufficiently discovered before them? Shall not my carpenter draw as satisfactory a right angle in sleeping ignorance as great Euclid in all the pride of his waking science? And if the angle can be had without the science, why should thought be cultivated, or the pain of thought endured, to have it? So therefore, in every department of civilized life, the same pattern recurs: the apprentice inherits, the journeyman repeats, the master bequeathes. The roles are distinguishable. The one constancy is the sleep of the soul. For the pattern will depend always on the same principle—the reduction of culture to formula. And it will produce always the same result—the substitution of ritual for renewal.

I would not be thought to disparage the power of craft that was engrossed in my neighbor's hand. Into that hand was entered, out of old and patient discipline, a power of effective art that mine has not and shall never acquire. His hand was consort to the chisel and companion to the pine. He could, by an alliance of sympathy with nature, make materials respond to idea, command form from the uncomplaining oak, implant purpose in alien things, so that the inhospitable earth respired with an inward meaning, *his* meaning, in answer to his sovereign act. Therefore, let no one who has not an equal honesty disparage carpenters. Until a man has built the roof that covers his own head, he cannot afford contempt; once he has built his roof, he will not allow it.

Nevertheless, admitting all of the just claims of my neighbor's craft, even allowing all of the melancholy limitations of the artless intellect, I would not exchange my geometry for his formula. The reason for this stubborn disregard of the advantages of simplicity is my conception not indeed of right angles but of right education. The power of an educated man cannot be thought to reside in the sterile capacity of repeating a formula which another has discovered; it resides in the productive capacity of repeating the discovery, of renewing the insight upon which any claim to independent mastery is grounded. The guild tradition is powerful to maintain standards, powerless to create them. It is founded essentially on imitation. An apprentice seeks to reproduce in his own practice the standard of performance he finds realized in the example of his master. Inevitably he will imitate. He will imitate with understanding if possible; but he will imitate without understanding if necessary. Understanding is nothing essential to his purpose, for his purpose is to secure a quality of performance not a style of mind. Let the example imitated be right, the reasons for its rightness may be left to the care of those whose business is reasons. For the craftsman, whose business is production, it is sufficient that the same product can be had, the same practice guaranteed, the same needs served, without reasons. The great and simple aim of the guild tradition, as the guild conceives it, is not to discipline our critical powers but precisely to make them superfluous, to spread right performance beyond the accidental limits of great talent or true opinion.

The guild tradition provides all of the benefits of a critical intelligence without the inconvenience of its exercise. That is why, of all of the inventions of legendary Daedalus, this pattern of social transmission is surely the greatest demonstration of his cunning. Daedalus discovered how to transmit intelligence without assuming any capacity for it in his sons. Icarus flies in every generation on borrowed wings; therefore, in every generation he is anonymously expendable. If he drowns, the race of artisans is less by one; but the stock of intelligence in the guild tradition is undiminished, since nothing depended on the presence of Icarus, and nothing is altered, alas, by his absence. Icarus is always replaceable for the reason that his power is always borrowed. The one person who is not replaceable, whose identity counts because his power is unborrowed, is Daedalus himself. He alone actively creates tradition—produces the formulas, establishes the routines, invents the techniques, which the passive generations draw upon. If on occasion, unpredictably, he reappears, resurrected in the guild of industry in a James Watt or an Eli Whitney, or in the guild of intellect in a Darwin or an Einstein or a Freud, his presence reverberates through all the earth, for men are at once aware that ordinary masters are to him as their raw apprentices are to themselves. They are peers not of him but only of each other. His mastery is original, theirs tributary and derived; and the tradition that suffices to account for their performances will not account for his. A new Daedalus comes always in spite of the guild tradition, never because of it, and to understand and supply the conditions of his emergence is the revolutionary function of the university in our society.

In the effort to liberate the Daedalus that is implicit in our powers the university puts a generation upon the permanent frontier of the most benignant revolution that mankind knows. In it lies the whole difference between education and training, between prophecy and priesthood, between the power of covenant and the power of ritual, in human affairs.

Therefore, when in the burdened solitude of my study I find myself reflecting upon the failures and divisions and conflicts of our inherited social institutions, I have learned to set a special value on this unheroic encounter with my carpenter. For I am persuaded that in him and me, poised there aloft on stepladders at either end of a timber, were brought together the two major patterns of social inheritance in human life. The first pattern is my carpenter's, which I call the *pattern of the guild*. The second is the inquisitive pattern, the pattern implicit in the question "Why?" which he forbade me, at least on his time, to practice or to dignify. There is no commonly accredited name for it. Let us call it the *pattern of the university*.

I should perhaps say at once that I do not in counterposing the guild and the university mean to diminish the one or to magnify the other. The pattern of the university appears, at times with an astonishing transparency, in the shop, the factory, and the forge. And the pattern of the guild appears, God knows, in the university, where sometimes it seems the pattern of the university appears not at all. In the twelfth century, when the first universities arose in France and Italy, the community of scholars was in fact, in the eye of the law, a special form of guild. But the term "university," which in English we restrict to the community of scholars, was then unrestricted. In the language of the Roman law *universitas* means simply "corporation," a corporation of any kind; and when the term was originally applied to the company of scholars, the idea of a collective person, of an artificial society permanent beneath the comings and goings of its individual members—or, as the sonorous old phrasing of the Dartmouth charter has it, of "one body corporate and politic, in deed, action, and name"—was all that was understood.[6] The *universitas* was the scholar's corporation—originally at Paris a guild of masters, at Bologna a guild of students, at Montpellier a guild of the two groups conjoined.[7] The term names their legal estate, not their intellectual commission, and if scholars were disposed then as now to interest themselves in the sense and direction of their corporate undertaking, in the idea of a concert, or philosophical commonwealth, of the sciences and the arts, that at all events was not what they sought to convey by the term "university."[8]

But for my own part I intend by the guild and the university neither the legal estate nor the intellectual commission. I intend, on the contrary, to direct attention to *two patterns of social inheritance*. These patterns are recognizable even beyond the formal limits of the guild and the university. They recur in fact, as we shall see, in every domain of social life. If, therefore, in order to name them, I single out the special domains in which they are most familiarly known, it must be understood that my interest is more general than my terms. Abelard worked in the pattern of the university though the University of Paris disowned him; Peter Lombard worked in the pattern of the guild though the university made him professor and adopted his textbook.

By the pattern of the university and the pattern of the guild I mean to distinguish between two kinds of tradition, between active and passive inheritance, in the relation of fathers and sons.

A person inherits *actively* if in entering into his inheritance he appropriates the principle that enabled its author to produce it; a person inherits *passively* if in entering into his inheritance he takes to himself the product but leaves the principle of production unappropriated. A passive inheritor acquires an *outward increase;* an active inheritor acquires, besides this increase, an *essential patrimony.* The difference is confirmable in overt behavior. An active beneficiary is capable of reconstituting his inheritance if the outward increase were lost; a passive beneficiary is not.

That is why the tradition of the university is socially so extraordinary a phenomenon. It performs the same function, it transmits the same rule of 3-4-5, as the oral tradition of the guild. But it has transformed the meaning of inheritance and the capacity of those who inherit.

An active tradition proceeds always from a demand for justification: its principle is criticism; its appeal is to evidence. A passive tradition proceeds from a demand for conservation: its principle is imitation; its appeal is to precedent. But this language is elliptical. It is never the tradition that is active or passive; it is we who are active or passive in it.

My carpenter inherits passively. He repeats the rule of 3-4-5 which his master repeated identically before him and which his apprentice shall repeat identically after him. The rule is their ritual, the ritual indefinitely resumed that binds together the succession of their generations in a universal priesthood. All alike are priests celebrant in a tradition without prophecy, the tradition of Aaron not of Moses, which they have received in pure passion of inheritance out of Egypt. With the rule my carpenter employs I find no fault. It is grounded, as we know, on a truth the generality of which is beyond his conception or his care. Its rectitude is for his purposes sufficiently confirmed by its visible utility in his quick act. Practically it works; therefore he works by it. His fateful omission is that he works by it but never at it. He is *active in the employment but passive in the system,* and the system owns him, tyrannizes in a secret dominion that condemns him to labor, as it condemns his society to dwell, a stranger in his father's house.

The factory system has in our day displaced the old guilds, but it has left the latent pattern, the pattern of passive inheritance that presided in the acts of the guildsman, untouched. The one difference is that in the factory system the passivity of the worker is no longer decently concealed. If my carpenter's T square will hold its right angle even when my carpenter sleeps, then it will be found to matter not at all who holds the T square, or in fact draws the angle, when he wakes. The angle may be had independently of his personal agency, or of the skill in his hand, or of the trade secrets in his head. Such is the significance of that simple mechanic T square he has fashioned for himself. His problem, once solved, is permanently solved. The solution has been objectively deposited in the tool, and the use of the tool is indefinitely transferable. The tool will in the hand of any laborer supply mechanically what formerly was supplied only by a conscious compliance with the discipline of the rule. My carpenter may therefore employ laborers to do ignorantly in his place the very acts that formerly demanded his time, his sensitive art, and his undivided critical attention. The factory system is at bottom founded on this delegableness of the physical performance to passive agents, that is, to persons who are active in the employment but passive in the system. It depends on our capacity, by means of tools, to extract the products of eminent skill from the unskilled; in short, to extract those products from passive laborers whose tools enable them, without craft, without understanding, and even without intention, to extend the benefits of other men's art.

The factory system has taken from the ancient guildsman the rituals of his oral tradition and with an eye to essentials absolved him of all offices of priesthood in the interests of production. In our society the transmission of rules is delegated to the corporation, the passion is reserved to the man, and all apprenticeship is permanent.

The pattern of the guild is the simple paradigm of all passively inherited culture. It is by no means limited to the traditions of the shop. The guild system of industry has disappeared from our society. But it is impossible to conceive a culture in which the function of cumulation and transmission once enacted by the guild is not preserved. The function *must* recur. For there never has been a society, and never will be one, that could afford to reflect critically upon all parts of its life at once. A human society, as my carpenter impatiently reminded me, is always constrained to hold aloft the other end of the timber; it must hold both ends aloft at once. Therefore, always for the majority of its acts, and sometimes for all of them, a society relies on custom, on old precedents and dignities and settled forms, which it has passively inherited and never thought to justify. A society will attempt to justify its established habits on one condition only, that one part of its array of social habits is in conflict with another; and in mending its disarray it will proceed invariably upon a principle of parsimony, of least change. It will allow no change beyond the least that is necessary in order to restore old slumber. The pattern of the guild is the most profoundly conservative structure in human history.

In our culture the pattern of the guild has been the avowed school of all of the established trades; but it has been the school also of the professions and the priesthoods, all of which behave for the majority of their acts (sometimes without awareness, always without confession) according to the same principle. In scientific institute, in court of law, in the political forum, in church, in school, in literature, music, and the arts, in all of society's gravest and most solemn precincts the pattern of passive inheritance shows itself. Political arrangements and economic practices, every ritual dispensation of religion, every fixed procedure of the law, all idioms of language, all forms and genres of art, the whole range of social conventions that subsist by routine beyond the reach of the critical faculty or by unarraigned habit beyond the election of the quickened moral consciousness, are transmitted by it. Wherever in the manifest life of society the status of men, or of classes of men, is determined by ascription, the pattern is at work. In what used to be known as scholasticism—the name for it in our season is methodology—the pattern invades the university itself and there presides in the inflexible stereotypes of thought and reflection, in the concealed assumption and the undisclosed category, that obscure the university's critical path and free commission.[9]

Why does the pattern thus intrude itself, even where it is least admitted and in principle disowned? Always for the same reason—that we are unable in practice, even the toughest advocates of the spirit of science among us, to do without it. The transfer of civilization is too urgent, our liability to error too omnipresent and fateful, our understanding too painfully limited to allow us in matters that touch our fundamental expectations to put thought before habit. Normally, we think only where habit fails; in a world in which habit perfectly succeeded there would be no thought at all. When a man claims to walk by sight in any connection, he needs reminding that he walks by ordinary disheveled faith in a thousand others he omits to notice or has forgotten to mention. He yields gratefully like ourselves, for all the larger constancies of his life, to the sustaining force of custom, familiar belief, established precedent, and old authority. When René Descartes, adopting doubt as his method, professes to reject all of his passively inherited former beliefs, he tacitly depends on the constable and his maidservant to preserve the peace out of doors and the fire in his hearth.

The pattern of the guild exhibits itself, in short, wherever in the inheritance of one generation from another we permit ourselves to substitute formula for principle, routine for insight, or ritual for covenant. The guild is the sphere of the customary in human life; the pattern of the guild is simply the mode of social transmission by which custom is conveyed.

All societies employ the pattern, societies the most advanced as well as societies the most primitive. A society perfectly primitive employs no other pattern. That precisely is what we mean by its primitiveness. The primitiveness of a society has nothing to do with the intricacy or the sophistication of its inheritance. Its primitiveness consists in its mode of inheritance, in the priestly passivity of its generations. A primitive society endures, if it endures at all, by ritual imitation of itself. Its moral task, the only task it will permit itself to see, is the bare regeneration of the forms that the past has conferred upon it. It admits but one option, either to repeat itself or to die. Repetition or extinction, that is the sole alternation which its vision of its destiny allows. Therefore, effectively, its life is concluded as soon as it is begun. Its present generation is always a redundancy, the idle replica of every other, in a perpetual renaissance that knows no reformation.

This stasis of mere culture is so profound a tendency of the human world that we fail to see in it an arrest of civilization. In simple societies—in the society of the Hopi Indian—the arrest will be transparent; in complex societies—in Egypt or Byzantium—it will conceal itself beneath an outward show of golden plenitude and large peace. The stasis of culture is nevertheless, in the one case as in the other, a form of social pathology, the lapse of a society from its station in history, its descent from a distinctively human to a merely natural condition. For the human condition is essentially historical. To be human *is* to be historical, to confront historical options, to take upon oneself the risk of constituting in the face of nature a creative evolution of which nature knows nothing.

An animal society—the society of the anthill or the hive—repeats itself for the reason that it has no other option. Immune to inward transformation, it is exposed to every outward transformation that challenges its own adequacy to endure. Its pattern is perfectly inflexible, as indelible as instinct, as fateful as gender. Its survival or extinction is therefore unilaterally determined by the action of the environment upon it. If the chances of the environment permit its survival, the society endures; if the chances of the environment forbid its survival, the society perishes. Such is the unqualified abjectness of its estate in nature. An animal society is not given to arbitrate the pattern it employs or to reconstitute the relevance of the pattern to the conditions it meets. This circumstance is the observable fact that I intend in saying that an animal society is beyond history. Its inheritance is purely passive; therefore, effectively, it is beyond tragedy. Its inheritance is its fate.

A primitive human society approximates to the same condition. It is, like an animal society, beyond history. But it is beyond history by historical default; by its own act of omission it has put itself there. A primitive society is a society in historical relapse, self-immolated and slumbering in a dry chrysalis of custom. It waits for release. It waits ignorant that the metamorphosis which custom shelters can be had only by a renewal of artifice, which custom forbids. For so long as a primitive society is required to meet only ordinary challenges, its inherited patterns will suffice. But the utility of such patterns depends always at last upon the perduring sameness of the conditions in which the society is placed. If these conditions change, the routine responses whose usefulness was once assured become then a primitive society's vain ritual, pattern divorced from meaning, which, if permanently uncriticized, will become the society's condemnation, the tragic inward source of its historical decline and fall.

The image of Sisyphus toiling with his stone is commonly mistaken for an image of the human condition. Properly, it is an image only of the guild mentality. Sisyphus is the guildsman in us all. He thinks he wants release from futility. What really he wants is analysis. Jove gives him a rock and a summit and the not unreasonable commission of bringing them together. But Sisyphus insists on treating the stone as an incorrigible integer. Therefore, he repeats the same act endlessly and condemns himself. The damnation of Sisyphus lies not in the severity of the task but in the inflexibly primitive intelligence of the laborer. Had he thought to break his stone into cubes and bear the parts separately, he would have served out his brief sentence in a day.

3. THE PATTERN OF THE UNIVERSITY

When the Psalmist asks, "What is man, that thou art mindful of him?" it will be evident to anyone who understands the question that its demand is not satisfied by the biologist's answer: "Man is the mammal identified in the species *Homo sapiens*." The fault with that answer is not that it wants truth. Its fault is that its truth fails to respond to the question that is asked. The answer describes man's fact; the question asks to know, on the contrary, his moral possibility, his proper commission and last calling, that he should count himself elect in the earth.

In just the same way, when we ask, "What is a university?" the sense of our question is not satisfied by soliciting a description of the *de facto* behavior of universities in the American scene. Circumstantially, as an external observer would describe the institution of the university in America, the university is this combination of loftiness and triviality, of sense and nonsense, of purity and compromise, which we who labor in it are party to. But that answer, though true, is not the truth that excites the surmise and supplies the motive of serious men who have put the question. We want to know what belongs to the idea of a university, what a university *would be* if it were ever to realize its proper calling in the American community.

What, then, in this sense—in the sense of its calling—is a university? I answer very simply, the organ of active inheritance in human society. *A university is the gathering of society's critical powers in order to liberate all of its other powers.*

Such is the moral seriousness of the idea of a university. Wherever that idea is permitted to operate, the university undertakes a public commission, the critical function of active inheritance in our society. The university can never therefore be rid of the fundamental questions which concern the objects of government, the meaning of wealth, and the aims of education. But neither can it be ever free from its commerce with the coke oven and the cattle stall. Repository and last guardian of all of society's larger life, its proper office is a free criticism. Conscientious in the root sense,[10] it is the institutional correlate of Emerson's conception of the scholar, "the delegated intellect," "Man Thinking."

That is not, however, as we all know, the institution we in fact meet, cleanly and perspicuously, in historical actuality. The institution we meet is a new phenomenon, the phenomenon Clark Kerr has described as the modern "multiversity."[11] And I must for a moment dwell upon this conception, since there is no person living who does not directly or indirectly experience its effects.

The university, as it has in fact evolved in American life, does not constitute a single universe of discourse. It is not in fact a universe at all; it is a multiverse, the ecological product of all of the miscellaneous forces—economic, political, medical, military, and social—that impinge upon it from without. The modern multiversity has no essential character of its own, no proper calling or commission which it is obliged in responsibility to realize or in trust to preserve. It is simply a loose assemblage of alien enterprises repeating the fragmentations and mirroring the contests that belong to the torn fabric of society beyond it. " 'The Idea of a Multiversity,' " says Clark Kerr, "has . . . its reality rooted in the logic of history. It is an imperative rather than a reasoned choice among elegant alternatives."[12] Its authentic virtue is that it responds to our live purposes. But these purposes, in it as in us, are very imperfectly integrated or reconciled. Individually, they make sense;

their combination eludes design. The multiversity is an aggregation of accidents fathered in the dark, an aggregation that interest has produced and ignorance has maintained and society has charged university presidents somehow to manage.[13]

When, in 1872, Daniel Coit Gilman accepted the presidency of the University of California, he found it important to draw a distinction between a university and a polytechnic institute. He favored the former; it is quite clear that the latter is what he got, and what after a century we still have. Clark Kerr's account of it is regrettably accurate, accurate not only for the University of California over which he himself (not without heroism) in his own time presided, accurate for other land-grant universities as well, accurate for all major universities of our day, including the Johns Hopkins University that Gilman founded.

The idea of a multiversity describes the accident of a profession, not the office and obligation of a society in search of itself. The problem that consumes the energies of all contemporary administrations is not how to mend the accident of the path we are on but how to accommodate it. Is it not enough that the university has been found in the twentieth century to have its uses? Therefore, shall not even its omissions be dignified and its defaults excused when its performances are so fatefully visible on every hand?

That is the pattern of the guild in the modern university. In the university as elsewhere, the pattern of the guild has an unimpeachable utility, and it is never to be taken lightly. But the truth is that this conception of the university fails even in its own terms, even in terms of "the uses of the university" that it rightly honors and obediently serves.

The modern scholar is active in the employment but passive in the system. The system distributes his labors according to the pattern of the guild. This pattern is faultlessly efficient in dividing the labors that we do: it is perfectly silent concerning any labor that by negligence we leave undone. The mechanical result is that the modern university has become the prisoner of its own departments. It has vacated its critical commission and exchanged, for the poor pottage of Esau, the public argument. Of all public institutions it is, with respect to the organization of its own enterprise, the least critical, the least well ordered, the least ready to respond to its integral commission.

The university is but society's instrument and tool for the pursuit of ends which not it, but society, has chosen. Yet the society that creates the university in its midst, and sustains the university by its support, is not competent, except in the broadest terms, to define its program. Society may, since the university is its creature, place a veto on any of its acts or suspend its acts entirely. But in this it is prepared to govern the university only negatively. What positively the university shall do, what its positive acts shall be, society leaves undefined, for the reason that it is not itself competent to define those acts and has created the university to act for it to that purpose.

To look to the uses of the university is not, as we have allowed ourselves to believe, to run contrary to Cardinal Newman's great proposition, that "there is a knowledge worth possessing for what it is, and not merely for what it does."[14] That sentence of Newman's has become, in the twentieth century, the last stay and support of the scholar in defending his enterprise. But the distinction of science from the uses of science, of understanding from practice, though philosophically correct, has been permitted to deflect analysis from the institution that is designed to cultivate it. The idea of a university is not a study of social absolution. The republic of scholars is not isolable from the body politic; neither shall we defend it by attempting to isolate it, on the holding of scholars that the pursuit of knowledge is a self-justifying activity. The general public will consent to that proposition only if it is educated to consent to it, only if it is shown that in the risks of a free scholarship its own freedom is extended.

Scholarship has become in fact a public office in the American commonwealth. Its commission remains public even when, in agreement with the pluralist premises of American educational institutions, its executants perform their labors under private auspices. What are the *de facto* conditions that circumscribe the role of the delegated intellect in American life? The university is its own first problem. I propose to deal with the social foundations of the scientific community—with the place of free inquiry in the political order, with the legitimacy of the self-governing professions, with the relations of science and government, with the social accountability of the scholar, and with the function of the higher learning in the education of a democracy.

NOTES

1. Cf. George N. Rainsford, *Congress and Higher Education in the Nineteenth Century* (Knoxville: University of Tennessee Press, 1972), pp. 93–95: "The lack of great public enthusiasm for the Morrill-Wade Act, considering its enormous impact, is one of the ironies of history. Lincoln signed it without comment on its merits. Even Horace Greeley, one of the chief supporters of the measure, declared he would be satisfied if only five schools were founded under its terms." See also Earle D. Ross, *Democracy's College: The Land-Grant Movement in the Formative Stage* (Ames: Iowa State College Press, 1942), pp. 66–67, and Frederick Rudolph, *The American College and University, A History* (New York: Vintage Books, 1962), pp. 247–263.

2. Francis Wayland, *Report to the Corporation of Brown University, On Changes in the System of Collegiate Education, Read March 28, 1850,* in *American Higher Education, A Documentary History,* edited by Richard Hofstadter and Wilson Smith (Chicago: The University of Chicago Press, 1961), vol. II, pp. 482–483.

3. John Fischer describes the move to the cities as "a migration of epic proportions." During the fifteen years prior to 1968, more than 10 million made the move. "A shift of population on this scale makes the Goths' incursion into the Roman Empire look like a Sunday outing. . . . 84 percent of our population is now crowded into only 212 metropolitan areas; less than 5 percent remains on farms." John Fischer, *Vital Signs, U.S.A.* (New York: Harper and Row, 1975), pp. 5–6.

"When Emerson spoke to a Massachusetts cattle fair in 1858," writes Allan Nevins, "he took as title 'The Man with the Hoe'; his farmer was still a manual worker. But that same year McCormick manufactured nearly 4,100 reapers." *The State Universities and Democracy* (Urbana: University of Illinois Press, 1962), p. 14, n.4.

4. Cf. Don K. Price, *Government and Science, Their Dynamic Relation in American Democracy* (New York: New York University Press, 1954), p. 42: "In the mid-nineteenth century there was no systematic relationship between a Joseph Henry, who was developing the theory of electromagnetism in the ivory towers of Princeton University and the Smithsonian Institution, and a Thomas Edison, who was applying this theory to commercial purposes. The scientist and the inventor were two entirely different classes of people; they lived and worked in quite different institutions and took pride in being different from each other. During the twentieth century, however, all this has been changed. The process of invention by the ingenious Yankee mechanic was changed into the business of scientific development, in which organized teams of scientists—as in the great Bell and General Electric laboratories—converted new scientific theory into practical application."

5. Cf. John F. A. Taylor, *The Masks of Society, An Inquiry into the Covenants of Civilization* (New York: Appleton-Century-Crofts, 1966), pp. 99–125.

6. The Latin that corresponds to our restricted use of the term "university" is *studium*, or more explicitly, where the institution encompassed the major faculties (arts, theology, civil and canon law, medicine), *studium generale*, "an association of masters and scholars established in some place with the intention to study the sciences." (Alfonso X El Sabio, *Las Siete Partidas o Libro de las leyes* [1263], vol. II, p. xxxi, quoted in Helene Wieruszowski, *The Medieval University* [Princeton, N.J.: Van Nostrand, 1966], p. 184). Thus, the phrase *universitas magistrorum et scholarium studii Parisiensis* means "the guild (*universitas*) of masters and scholars of the University (*studii*) of Paris."

7. At Bologna the organization of masters was entitled *collegium doctorum*, that is, "the faculty assembly." The assembly was without consequent authority. The *studium* was run by the guild of students. Cf. Lowrie J. Daly, *The Medieval University, 1200–1400* (New York: Sheed and Ward, 1961), p. 47: "When Napoleon captured Bologna in June, 1796, the nations [the student guilds] and their officers were definitely dispersed. In 1798, for the first time in probably more than six hundred years of continued existence, the University of Bologna had a rector who was not a student but a professor."

8. Cf. Charles Homer Haskins, *The Rise of Universities* (New York: Holt, 1923), p. 14: "Historically, the word university has no connection with the universe or the universality of learning; it denotes only the totality of a group, whether of barbers, carpenters, or

students did not matter." See also Hastings Rashdall, *The Universities of Europe in the Middle Ages,* edited by F. M. Powicke and A. B. Emden, (Oxford: Clarendon Press, 1895), vol. I, pp. 6–7.

The proposition that "a University should teach universal knowledge" is a distinct thesis, the thesis of Newman's "Second Discourse": see John Henry Cardinal Newman, *The Idea of a University,* edited by C. F. Harrold (New York: Longmans, Green, 1947 [1852]), p. 19. Cf. Hugo of Saint Victor: "The seven liberal arts form an integrated whole; they are in mutual need of each other in the sense that if one is lacking, the rest are not sufficient to make a philosopher. Those who disregard the inner unity of the arts, selecting some of them for study and believing that in these they can be perfect without the help of the others, are utterly mistaken. . . ." (*Didascalion,* quoted in H. Wieruszowski, op. cit., p. 128).

9. The keenest perception of this circumstance in contemporary literature is to be found in Thomas S. Kuhn's extraordinary essay, *The Structure of Scientific Revolutions* (Chicago: The University of Chicago Press, 1962 [1968]).

10. "When Karl Jaspers suggested something new in Europe, a technological faculty in the university, he did it for a most un-American reason. He explicitly did not do it because he was concerned that his country, or Europe, was falling behind in the production of engineers. . . . He did it because he wanted to put technology in its place. He wanted to bring it within the circle of knowledge and not leave it to technicians. He wanted to subject other disciplines to interaction with it and it to interaction with other disciplines. His summary statement was: 'The university must face the great problem of modern man: how out of technology there can arise the metaphysical foundation of a new way of life which technology has made possible.' " Robert M. Hutchins, "The University in America" (Santa Barbara, Calif.: Center for the Study of Democratic Institutions, 1967), pp. 7–8.

11. Clark Kerr, *The Uses of the University* (Cambridge, Mass.: Harvard University Press, 1963).

12. Ibid., p. 6.

13. Ibid., p. 9: "How did the university happen? No man created it; in fact, no man visualized it. It has been a long time coming about and it has a long way to go."

14. Newman, op. cit., p. 101.

3.

THE U.S. SUPREME COURT, THE SCHOLAR, AND THE DEMOCRATIC FAITH

1. THE OBLIGATIONS OF A PROFESSIONAL

It must be confessed that the academic profession is in all of its external relations, in all relations touching the conditions of its public performance, the most ignorant of the learned professions. The scholarly profession has never studied for its purposes, what the traditionally accredited professions of medicine and law have long since mastered for theirs, how to reconcile in one person the independence of a professional and the obedience of an employee.

An academic protests his freedom exactly where another professional—a physician, a lawyer, or an engineer—would in simplicity confess his duty and go silently about doing it. A medical doctor would never think to ask his patient, as an academic asks society, to approve his freedom. On the contrary, the medical doctor asks his patient to approve the performance of those acts that have on technical grounds been found *necessary*, and that are therefore *obligatory*, if the patient's interest is to be served. Freedom is reserved to the patient, not to the professional who ministers to him; it lies where the risk lies, and may never in a professional performance be permitted to lie elsewhere. To the physician belongs, not freedom, but obligation only, the burden of one who acts responsibly in another's behalf. The physician requires of himself specific performances which the patient has not the technical information to ask of him; he must exercise his own discretion in connections the patient is not equipped to understand. His discretionary freedom is nevertheless strictly regulated by his obligation to the patient whose interest he has made his own. That is why, in ordinary practice, if the patient should die beneath his hand, the physician is not thought to have offended against the peace of society. In the right performance of his role, the physician is presumed to work by an implicitly delegated authority.[1] He does but execute the acts the patient would himself have authorized had he possessed the instructed powers which the professional brings to him.

A scholar's relation to society is at bottom the same. He stands professionally related to society as the medical doctor stands related to his patient, or an attorney to his client, or an architect to the patron who commissions him. The nomenclature varies with the calling, but in all of these cases the same basic paradigm recurs—the obligation of a trained and certified professional exercising his powers in the interest of a client who retains him.

Like all professionals, the scholar is implicated in what he regards as a fiduciary role. He executes a trust, he works by a delegated authority, in which not his own but the interest of others presides. The freedom of scholarship is not, as the scholar construes it, a license for him to think as he likes; it is, on the contrary, an imperative addressed to all scholars who labor in pursuit of a commonwealth of learning to put liking aside, to disclaim arbitrariness of judgment, to subordinate private belief to the force of evidence openly published and freely assembled. The emblem of the scholar's activity is not the book he writes but the corporate and public "circle of learning," literally the encyclopedia (*enkyklios paideia*), to which it contributes. In a word, the scholar enacts the duties of what he conceives to be a public office. He therefore claims to himself a public officer's immunity, so long as he acts within the delegated powers of his office, to proceed without interference wherever the search for truth might lead him.

I do not mean by this description to recite an apology. I have no delusions concerning the self-abnegations of scholars, nor do I claim for the breed any eminent dignity, any special disinterestedness or devotion to public service, that the most skeptically detached observer would not in candor admit them to have. If the practicing scholar works *de iure* in the interest of others, he works also *de facto* manifestly in his own. Nothing is gained by neglecting or attempting to conceal the circumstance that professionals—historians, men of letters, and scientists as well as lawyers, physicians, and engineers—grunt and sweat under a weary life in order that they might eat. Their intellectual eminence does not absolve them of any single consequence of their economic condition, and in this all-too-human condemnation they are like the least of their clients, like all ordinary hewers of wood and drawers of water, who are obliged in the ruck of the marketplace, beneath the common sun, to gain their livelihood by exchanging services for wages.

All of this we may frankly acknowledge and even, with that agreeable self-mortification that has become sentimentally fashionable in our day,[2] insist on. It is nevertheless important, if we would understand the scholar's claim to freedom, to mark the difference in any profession properly so called between the fiduciary relationship that is essential to it and the economic relationship that is contingent and accidental. A medical doctor performs his essential function when he works to heal his patient; whether, in fact, in working to heal his patient, he also makes a living for himself is, for the strict purposes of medicine, an accident. The making of a living may be in point of fact the doctor's primary motive for engaging in his practice; but it is not essential to his professional estate. He would remain equally professional if his living came to him from independent sources and the practice of healing were his charity or his penance or his servitude. "Sometimes," says Hippocrates, "give your services for nothing. . . . For where there is love of man, there is also love of the art."[3] In the prayer of Moses Maimonides the same awareness of essential commission recurs: "Do not allow thirst for profit, ambition for renown and admiration, to interfere with my profession. . . . In the sufferer let me see only the human being."[4] Summoned to attend upon a patient, the physician need not pretend to be superior to his fee. He nevertheless governs himself, in the measure that he respects his role, according to the inherent obligations of his profession. Those obligations exact from him a ministration, not an altruism; a technical performance, not a quality of heart or mind. Suppose the performance to be fitted to the patient's need, suppose the outward act to be technically right, it will matter not at all whether the private inward motive of the doctor is the well-being of his patient or the well-being of himself, a reverence for life in Lambaréné or a reverence for profit in Hoboken.

Let the fiduciary function that is essential to a profession (as the practice of healing is essential to medicine, or the practice of counseling to law) be called the *inherent function* of that profession. And let any other function, any function that is (like the making of a living for the professional) consistent with the practice of the profession but not essential to it—let any such function be called an *adherent function*. Then it will be evident that in ordinary practice the role of a professional is describable in two ways. In terms of its inherent function, it will be described as the obligation of the professional to what I may call a *privileged beneficiary*, that is, to a beneficiary whose interest he must allow to take precedence in any right performance of the function. Such is the obligation, for example, of a teacher to his student, of an attorney to his client, of a doctor to his patient, or of an architect to his patron. In each case, in the measure that teaching or legal counsel or healing or the delegation of design is understood, the preeminence of the claims of a privileged beneficiary, of a beneficiary whose interest supersedes all others, is also understood.

But each of these professions may also be described in terms of its adherent functions. In this description each will appear as the obligation of a professional to a merely *contingent beneficiary*. Such is the relation, for example, of a teacher of students to his corporate employer, or of a researcher in the scientific community to the government foundation that supports his work, or of a lawyer to the civil rights organization that underwrites the costs of defending his client. There then occurs, for one and the same professional, an obligation to a contingent as well as to a privileged beneficiary. What, in the ethic of a profession, is the force of the latter's privilege? Simply this, that in any conflict of inherent and adherent obligations with each other, the inherent obligation must prevail.

Before this resolution no one, I think, hesitates, and if the conduct of a profession had always this clean simplicity, the professions new and old would set for us none of the painfully perplexing moral problems that they do. The most intractable problems of a professional arise typically from a conflict of obligations, *both of which are inherent.* If a professor of medicine demonstrates a new surgical technique for the benefit of persons (students or colleagues) other than his patient, he acts then simultaneously in two distinguishable professional roles. He is teacher; he is physician; he is both at once. But the obligations he acknowledges are radically ambivalent. The obligation that is inherent with respect to one beneficiary, or one set of beneficiaries, is merely adherent with respect to the other. In the professor of medicine's role as teacher the students are privileged; in his role as physician the patient is privileged. Both obligations are inherent. Which obligation must take precedence if the need for a decision between them should arise? There can be no question that the patient's privilege commands the prior obedience. But it is clear that this decision is not made, and cannot be made, on merely professional grounds. It is a decision, not of medicine or of pedagogy, but of morals. That is the discovery which the modern consciousness has drawn from the testament of Nuremberg. The profession of medicine and the profession of teaching—at last all professions—fall under the constraint of a moral covenant that transcends them all alike.

Ordinarily, however, in the benign routine of the professions, such radical moral arrests do not occur. Inherent and adherent functions come together pacifically in the activity of one and the same professional, who conducts his affairs, without experienced tension, in an easy concurrence of the two roles. Preacher, teacher, scholar, physician, lawyer, engineer— each performs professionally in another's interest for a fee. All (though not all equally) are impervious to that artificial contempt that Socrates taught the Athenians to turn upon their professional teachers, those enterprising mercenaries of intellect whom he ironically called Sophists, that is to say, "wiseacres," "hucksters of wisdom." The most renowned of these teachers, the venerable Protagoras, whose dissident beliefs excited the remonstances of the young Socrates, professed, for a fee, to teach men virtue, and saw no indignity, having rendered what both he and his hearers accounted an honest service, in demanding to be paid for his pains. Asked to reconcile his fee with his freedom, this ancient trafficker in the market would no doubt have answered quite simply, in the manner of any modern professional, that the fee had nothing to do with the quality of his public service, though much with his private ability to go on rendering it. With respect to the latter Protagoras was, and was content that others should consider him, the frank party to an economic exchange, unashamed to demand for his ounce of discourse an ounce of fair return. It is not otherwise with modern professionals: they praise Socrates and imitate Protagoras. Louis Agassiz, invited by the French emperor to leave Harvard in order to improve his income in the service of France, replied laconically that he could not afford to waste time making money.[5] It was an admirable answer, and I wish I had said it. But I am told on excellent authority that this measure of intellectual austerity is perhaps original rather than representative even at Harvard; and it may be worth noting, historically, that the professor's asceticism, which renounced a strip of bacon with his egg in Paris, was not carried in Cambridge to the illiberal extreme of renouncing the egg as well.

It must not be supposed, however, that the two roles of the scholar—the inherent role of the professional and the adherent role of the employee—are always thus effortlessly reconciled. The easy peace of the established professions, the peace that enables a physician to accept his fee, or a lawyer his retainer, without thought of compromising the independence of his professional judgment, this peace has immemorially been denied to those who have, like Protagoras or Socrates himself, made thought their commission. In general, society reserves its formal employments, as it reserves its priesthoods, for those who will least disturb its slumber. It fires its critics as it fires its prophets, exactly in the measure of their originality, in the measure of their power to bring forth, unprompted, the heroic germinal ideas upon which all great transformations of human affairs are grounded. The city that killed Socrates had already banished Protagoras before him. The Athenians were undisturbed by the cupidity of the mercenary; they found unpardonable the independence of the thinker. Baruch Spinoza, to preserve inviolate the *libertas philosophandi* which he enjoyed privately as a lens grinder in the Hague, found it necessary to refuse a chair of philosophy that had been offered to him, with conditions attached, at the University of Heidelberg. In Spinoza's world, as in ours, the conditions of public service were on occasion inconsistent with the conditions of public employment. In America they are

sometimes inconsistent with the conditions even of a private
employment. *Cuius regio, eius scientia.* Or, as our blunt phrase
is, "The hand that writes the paycheck rules the school." Did
not Alexander Hamilton warn that "a power over a man's subsistence amounts to a power over his will"?[6] John Stuart Mill,
apprehensive lest the anonymous force of majority opinion be
found a greater tyranny than any force levied by a calculable
despot, reminded his countrymen that "men might as well be
imprisoned, as excluded from the means of earning their
bread."[7] A great part of the struggle for academic freedom in
the United States has been lived under the shadow of this conflict between the inherent and adherent roles of the scholar,
between his fiduciary function as a professional and his non-
fiduciary function as an employee. The adherent role of the
employee is the only role the public sees or chooses to take
into account as directly touching its proper interest. The
teacher is an employee who sells his services for wages. From
this circumstance the public has always concluded, and until
lately the courts have always agreed, that the right of deter-
mining what shall and shall not be taught must lie in the discretion of the employer. The public is at liberty to establish
the conditions of service to itself; and the teacher, it is everywhere easily assumed, is at liberty not to serve if he finds the
conditions arbitrary, unreasonable, or repugnant.

2. "THE ILLIMITABLE FREEDOM OF THE HUMAN MIND"

It is a mistake to suppose that the university in America has
arisen from the spontaneous private initiatives of scholars. Of
the earliest universities in medieval Europe this could perhaps
be claimed. The medieval universities in the oldest centers
proceeded from acts of incorporation of which scholars were
the authors, main beneficiaries, and first trustees. When in the
thirteenth century the emperor Frederick II founded the University of Naples to serve as a counterweight to the learning of
the Guelph city of Bologna, Bologna's venerable university
was already, without benefit of political intercessions, more

than a century old. So universally acclaimed was Bologna's authority in the Roman law that the emperor's grandfather, Barbarossa, had had no option but to summon its professors in order to define his own rights in Italy. The privilege Barbarossa granted at Roncaglia did but confirm at law a recognition that triumphant learning had won without it.

This description fails indeed to declare the real variety of forms that scholars themselves encountered in the oldest centers of learning. The legal community was at Bologna a corporation of students, at Paris a corporation of masters, at Montpellier a corporation that brought together both of these. Still, whether of masters or of students, communities of scholars they all were, and in each of them the object of incorporation was the same—to gain recognition of the rights of the academic community in relation to the larger community that fell beyond it.

Scholars had in those days the most urgent practical incentives for cultivating their community. Their motive was not, at least it was not at first, the advancement of learning. Their motive was security, the rudimentary support of civil rights. In the universal localism of the medieval towns, the primary guarantees of the civil law were jealously restricted in favor of the burghers. Unless a scholar was himself a native of the town or a person whose irresistible distinction had earned him the privileges of a citizen, his status at law was always precarious, in best times insecure, in worst times insupportable. In his individual capacity he could press no right, urge no defense, claim no protection beyond that which the public peace afforded or the condescension of the law court would allow. Of Bologna the learned Rashdall writes: "The conception of citizenship prevalent in the Italian republics was much nearer to the old Greek conception than that which prevails in modern states. Citizenship, which is with us little more than an accident of domicile, was in ancient Athens or medieval Bologna an hereditary possession of priceless value. The citizen of one town had, in the absence of express agreement, no civil rights in another. There was one law for the citizen; an-

other, and a much harsher one, for the alien."[8] The hand of
the creditor was permitted to reach, in the flight or insolvency
of the debtor, to the debtor's fellow countryman, whose only
error was that he was present and incarcerable, and had
money in his purse.[9] Even in France, where scholars were
privileged as clerks to be tried in ecclesiastical courts, it was
found necessary to instruct magistrates, in any case that involved a burgher as one of the litigants, not to allow custom
to override the written law.[10]

The great majority of scholars thus found themselves, except for their power of association, under the afflicting disa-
bilities of permanent aliens. "Exiles for the love of knowledge"
they called themselves; "wanderers for the cause of study"
they were called. They suffered all of the usual penalties and
disqualifications that have immemorially been visited upon
that special breed of exploitable humanity whom we describe,
in American public education, as "out of state." They came,
typically, from all quarters of Europe—from Germany, from
the Low Countries, from England, from Spain, from the provinces of France and the hill towns of Italy. They came very
much as Americans still come from all quarters of the nation,
settling themselves (until lately in forfeiture of their right to
vote) in the school towns of Massachusetts or Pennsylvania,
Michigan or California. And having come, the medieval
scholar stood, except for his membership in the scholars'
guild, solitary in the shadow of another's law, disarmed and
exposed, surrounded by importunate landlords and shopkeep-
ers, wine merchants and moneylenders, panderers and apoth-
ecaries, all of whom he dimly suspected of loving his purse
more than his person, the money in his hand more than the
learning in his head, his intelligible passion for women more
than his unintelligible passion for Aristotle. Therefore, spon-
taneously, by their own motion, the scholars organized, com-
posed a charter and established a corporation, and sought to
exact by combination a security that the careless town denied
to them as individuals.

In America the university has arisen from a different motive. The university in America is the creation, not of the scholar, but of the town. At no time in the life of the republic has the primary motive for the estabishment of an American institution of higher learning been a defense of the rights of scholars or a special solicitude for the freedom of their community as a sufficient good. On the contrary, the motive has everywhere been, quite simply, the advancement of the public interest. Men, some of them quite innocent of formal education, perceived the transforming utility of scientific enlightenment in pursuits that fell beyond the blank gates of the academy. They believed in the perfectibility of their society, and their foundations ran with their initiatives. If the scholar, then as now, responded to the intrinsic possibilities that were opened up, for him and others like him, in the interstices of the roles philanthropy had created and education had confirmed, he availed himself of an opportunity for professional association that no one had precisely intended.

Thomas Jefferson said of the university he labored to design that it was to be based on the "illimitable freedom of the human mind."[11] The phrasing was, as usual, in matters about which he greatly cared, unerringly right—as unerringly right as it was politically unsettling. What nation that claimed political sovereignty would ever thus dare to license its own critic? What established authority, uncompelled, would expose itself to the scandal of a permanent inquisition which it consented to support but refused to control? Yet that scandal was precisely what Thomas Jefferson intended by a university. "For here," he wrote, "we are not afraid to follow truth wherever it may lead, nor to tolerate any error, so long as reason is left free to combat it."[12]

Then as now, the real measure of toleration in a democratic society remained to be explored. But of this Jefferson was already fully persuaded, that the freedom needed for his brave experiment was the freedom he described—the freedom of the human mind, not the freedom of an academy. In Jefferson's vision of society, the freedom of the human mind is original and self-justifying. Politically, every other value must be held subordinate to this, since, given this, every other value will be generated out of the released energies of free men, but, without this, every other value is insecure.

> Invest me in my motley; give me leave
> To speak my mind, and I will through and through
> Cleanse the foul body of th' infected world. . . .[13]

The freedom of an academy has no such independent warranty. An academy is, after all, like law or government, a mere instrumentality of society. Established in the public interest, it has no justification whatever except as it may be shown to contribute to that interest. The freedom of the human mind is, on the other hand, that interest itself. Matrix and shelter of every other value, it is what all voluntary society is about, and any society that disparages or neglects it is by that omission condemned to impermanence. A presumed variety of freedom especially reserved for scholars—the kind of freedom we distinctively describe as academic—would therefore have puzzled Jefferson. It would have seemed to him (who once said if he could not go to heaven but with a party, he preferred not to go at all) an error of conception, a confusion of freedom with obligation, in which the public commission of the university was forgotten or misunderstood. For he refused to regard the pursuit of truth, as we have allowed ourselves to regard it, as the cultivation of a private garden. The employments of the scholar are not a monastic retreat from the tasks of society; they are not an aristocratic indulgence; they are public employments, an indispensable part of our social task, a gathering of society's critical powers in order to set free all of its other powers.

"I know," Jefferson wrote to William Jarvis, "no safe depository of the ultimate powers of the society but the people themselves; and if we think them not enlightened enough to exercise their control with a wholesome discretion, the remedy is not to take it from them, but to inform their discretion with education."[14] To George Ticknor, professor at Harvard, he observed: "We are not . . . rivals, but fellow-laborers in the same field, where the harvest is great, and the laborers few."[15] The interests of the man of affairs who founds a university, the interests of the man of thought who performs its offices— these interests, if at times they move separate, at last must intersect and join. At last they must coincide, for they have but one aim, the execution of a public trust, "the improvement of our country by science."[16]

Academics have never wearied of repeating Jefferson's declaration of the independence of the human mind. Their enthusiasm is easily understood. No other digest of their business so perfectly expresses the interior covenant of the scientific community or commands such unqualified consent among the scholars who populate it in one season and another. But it must be admitted that American scholars have failed to hold before themselves the presiding social purposes that animated Jefferson in his resolve to found, in Virginia, the first of our state universities. When political opposition to Thomas Cooper's religious opinions blocked the confirmation of his appointment, Jefferson suffered great chagrin. He regretted the loss of the free scholar, but he was unwilling to allow a sectarian difference to jeopardize the social good, and the freedom of the academy was made to yield to it. Modern faculties admit no such restraint upon their autonomy. They preserve unimpaired Jefferson's appreciation of the need for an unfettered scholarship; they neglect his vision of the place of scholarship in the public life. The result is that they have fallen into the disastrous error of supposing that the freedom of the university is a privilege instituted for the special benefit of scholars. They speak everywhere of the freedom, nowhere of the social function, of their community; therefore, by plain men, the freedom of their community is everywhere doubted, and its function nowhere understood. The American scholar has failed either to apprehend for himself or to communicate to others the fundamental affirmation of the community of scholars, that scholarship is a public office, and the scholar a public officer, performing by delegation the duties of a public trust.

Historically, the American community of scholars has

come to pass not by policy but by inattention. We have not begun with it; we have discovered it—like America itself— after the fact.

In the making of a new society in a new world the first need of those who arrived on our shores was to feed and shelter their society and to secure its physical safety. But the second need was, as all thoughtful men perceived, to conserve their moral achievement—to prepare teachers to educate their young, ministers to preach their gospel, lawyers to plead their rights, and physicians to heal their maladies. Therefore, deliberately, they conceived an institution equipped to perform these necessary offices, chartered it, empowered trustees to direct it, appointed a president to run it, and set for him the immediate first task of hiring scholars to man it.

The scholar who was hired to man it had from the beginning, in America, a systematically ambiguous status. The university is always in fact two communities—a collegial community of scholarship and a contractual community of employment. The scholar belonged to both. He was the certified local officer of a branch of learning; he was at the same time the paid employee of a lay corporation. Each of these roles generated its own set of obligations, and the two sets of obligations (since they fell upon the same person) had necessarily to be adjusted to each other. In ordinary times the adjustment took place without incident. But the times were not always ordinary; they were never ordinary if the life of thought was vigorous; and a whole history has unfolded from the circumstance that the scholar's certification proceeded from one source, his pay from another. Professionally, as he viewed his own commission, he was party to the covenant of a self-governing community of scholars, which extended beyond this or that petty precinct of his labors and even beyond the nation or generation in which his labors fell. Formally, however, as society interpreted his commission, he was an employee, the paid servant of a corporation that was governed not by scholars but by lay trustees. Every effort was made to smooth over the difficulties that were implicit in this arrangement. Academic etiquette required that the scholar be described as entering upon his duties by appointment rather than by hiring; he was paid a stipend or a salary, never wages; and it was doubtless useful to reflect that in the part of the vineyard assigned to his special care he more nearly resembled a managing steward than a domestic. Nevertheless, in spite of these civilizing concessions, in the eye of society he remained an employee. He was neither (like the twelfth-century guildsman) the author of the enterprise, nor in any special sense (like the distinguished first rector of the University of Virginia) its architect and overseer. If he claimed membership in a professional calling that was independent of his employment and that might in case of conflict take precedence over it, that at all events was not the judgment of his society, and it would not be long before men asked, on the one hand, by what right a servant should dare to hold opinions contrary to those of his master, and, on the other, what would happen to the illimitable freedom of the human mind if he were forbidden to do so.

In English universities, at least on the surface, the status of employee was admissible without prejudice to the freedom of scholarship. It is true that royal commissions discreetly conveyed the learned intentions of the royal mind; aberrant statutes were sometimes accommodatingly rewritten; oaths were required; and augmented stipends for heads of colleges ("those little living idols or monuments of monarchy," a contemporary of Oliver Cromwell called them) were not perhaps without effect. Ostensibly, however, Oxford and Cambridge arranged their affairs, without external interference, according to the usages of self-government inherited from the medieval guilds. Authority proceeded from the corporation, and the corporation was understood to coincide with the community of scholars, so that, at any rate in theory, no question could arise whether the scholar was free to speak and think as scholars spoke and thought. But the American scholarly community had not this formal independence as a class. For legal purposes, all of the primary controls of the teaching community emanated from the lay sources that provided its support and interpreted its social purposes. The right of government was unambiguously vested in a lay board of trustees, a collection of individuals artificially empowered to act as one person and, by virtue of its capacity to renew its own membership, to perpetuate itself through time, in John Marshall's phrase, "like one immortal being." Technically, the trustees were the corporation. But since the membership of the board was, except in its formal sessions, scattered abroad in the larger community from which it was drawn, the actual administration of the board's policies fell to the president, who by delegation managed between sessions in its place. Appointed by the trustees, privileged in their presence, plenipotentiary in their absence, the president exercised a continuous and visible authority. In fact if not in law, he *was* the college and was generally, both by the trustees and by the larger community, so regarded. The faculty was his creation, employed according to his recommendation, structured according to his lights, dissolvable at his displeasure. At its best, under a Witherspoon, an Eliot, or a Gilman, it might become an authentic community of scholars. But it did not begin as that, and this result depended gratuitously on the president's ability and judgment. The faculty membership was transient. Such community as it had, it had by secondary delegation and by sufferance. The community of scholars in all but the greatest of our institutions was an epiphenomenon, not the product of design, but an unpremeditated accident, which came to pass, if it came to pass at all, like the rainbow, in spite of anyone's intention.

3. OF SCHOLARSHIP AS A PUBLIC OFFICE

In American society the outward forms of privacy that belong to some of the most illustrious of our scholarly institutions obscure the public character of the services they perform. At a state institution the public commission of the scholar is confirmed by the auspices under which he works. But at a private institution—at Yale or Columbia, at Chicago or Stanford—we lose sight of the public commission in the splendor of the private endowment. The public objects of the university, which are consequent, are concealed by the private auspices, which are ceremonial. In America, as usual, nothing fits theory. The most vexatious incongruities appear between our social realities and our legal forms, and nowhere is the discrepancy so exaggerated as in the government of universities.

The ambivalence of privacy in the pattern of American institutions of higher learning has a long history. In 1819, in the Dartmouth College Case, it occupied the direct contemplation of the Supreme Court of the United States.[17] The question in contention was, whether Dartmouth College, whose charter had been challenged by the legislature of New Hampshire, was a public or a private corporation. Daniel Webster, speaking for the trustees, pleaded that the gravity of the principle at stake in the preservation of the Dartmouth charter far exceeded the importance of a small and easily vanquished literary establishment, that the principle was property—not literature, not education, not science or enlightenment, but the continuity of private rights and the sanctity of contract in American life. Chief Justice John Marshall was not unmoved. The learned jurist comforted the advocate and silenced his Republican enemies with the firm assurance that in the eye of the law a peppercorn is of sufficient value to found a contract. He wrote:

That education is an object of national concern, and a proper subject of legislation, all admit. That there may be an institution founded by government, and placed entirely under its immediate control, the officers of which would be public officers, amenable exclusively to government, none will deny. But is Dartmouth College such an institution? . . . Does every teacher of youth become a public officer, and do donations for the purpose of education necessarily become public property, so far that the will of the legislature, not the will of the donor, becomes the law of the donation?

The answer must of course be, No. For whether a teacher of youth becomes a public officer will depend always on the way in which the office is understood, and it may very well be that there are offices of science in which neither the will of the legislature nor the will of the donor, but the judgment of the scientist who is their paid employee, must be the law of the donation. What, it may be asked, has Euclid to do with donors, or Newton with trustees, or Shakespeare with the legislature of the State of New Hampshire?

But these were, for the time being, thoughts out of season; and Marshall (though his answer was also No) chose, in setting down his opinion, to attend rather to the contract than to the peppercorn. Dartmouth College is a chartered corporation, "a seminary of education, incorporated for the preservation of its property, and the perpetual application of that property to the objects of its creation." The Constitution of the United States forbids any state to pass a law that will impair the obligations of contract. The charter of Dartmouth College is within the letter of the Constitution a contract and falls beneath the shelter of this prohibition.

In consequence of this decision, the idea of a university in American society has for more than a century been buried in a property right.

Accustomed to believing that our legal forms are a reliable index of our social realities, we have permitted ourselves to assume that a university acquires its public or private character, not from the public purposes it is designed to promote, but from the public or private sources of its financial support. An institution like Dartmouth, since its charter declares it to be a private corporation, is therefore presumed to enact a private function. And that is no doubt, at some institutions, true. It is true of a convent. It is true of a privately segregated Mississippi school. Proprietary institutions formed for the sole purpose of inculcating the doctrines of a religious sect, of a political party, or of a class interest are private both in auspices and in object. But the social reality remains. Functionally, in spite of its legal claims to privacy, Dartmouth College performs in the life of our society a demonstrably public office. It is the private enactment of a public function, exactly as American Telephone & Telegraph (or, for that matter, General

Motors, or U.S. Steel, or International Business Machines) is the private enactment of a public function, that is to say, of a function which, if it were left undone by the private agency, would have then indispensably to be done by the public agency. The railroads of the nation wear this complication on their sleeve: their ownership is private, their function public; the ownership is extinguishable, the function is not. In all of these cases a too-exclusive attention to legal entitlements conceals the fiction in the law, the originality in the corporation, and the pluralism in the actual path of our society. The path, in education as in industry, has ceased to run with ownership; it runs with the effective demand of the society. We honor the demand and hope that the law will follow suit. In the life of intellect, provided the idea has been mastered, it matters not at all who owns the book.

In 1915, when the American Association of University Professors was founded, it was considered essential to set before the candid world the principles the new organization was instituted to defend. John Dewey, first president of the association, gave the charge of formulating such a statement of principles into the hands of a committee of fifteen members, the association's original Committee on Academic Freedom and Academic Tenure, an extraordinary constellation of some of the most eminent luminaries in American intellectual history. Edwin R. A. Seligman, distinguished economist of Columbia University, authority on public finance, editor of the *Encyclopaedia of the Social Sciences,* was named chairman; beside him sat Roscoe Pound of Harvard, Richard T. Ely of Wisconsin, and Arthur O. Lovejoy of Johns Hopkins. The committee produced a memorable document that has come to be known, in the history of the association, as *The 1915 Declaration of Principles.*[18] It is the purest sustained expression of professional principles in the American tradition.

The argument of the *Declaration* turns upon the distinction of a public and a private trust. A proprietary institution is one that is restricted by the terms of its endowment to the propagation of specific doctrines; its trustees are by law obliged to require of professors the advocacy of a partisanship—the dogmas of a sectarian religious belief, of an economic or political persuasion. A public institution is, on the contrary, "an intellectual experiment station," wedded to no prescribed body of doctrine. It may be, legally, founded on a private charter; it may be, economically, dependent on private support. But neither charter nor endowment is permitted to determine the path of inquiry or its conclusion. The institution is public for the reason that it enacts a public function, executes a public trust, and can without equivocation appeal for public support in return for its services.

What is the relation of trustees and professors in a proprietary institution? That of an ordinary business venture, the relation of master to servant, of employer to employee. The employee may be admitted into employment only by undertaking to make himself party to the sectarian or economic or political bias of those who have furnished the endowment. He may be arbitrarily dismissed when his opinions, however well-established in scholarly councils, run counter to the authorized doctrine.

What is the relation of trustees and professors in "an untrammeled institution of learning"? A relation necessarily grounded on an understanding of "the nature of the social function discharged by a professional scholar," to wit, "to deal at first hand, after prolonged and specialized technical training, with the sources of knowledge; and to impart the results of their own and of their fellow-scientists' investigation and reflection, both to students and to the general public, without fear or favor."

The lay public is under no compulsion to accept or to act upon the opinions of the scientific experts whom, through the universities, it employs. But it is highly needful, in the interest of society at large, that what purport to be the conclusions of men trained for, and dedicated to, the quest for truth, shall in fact be the conclusions of such men, and not echoes of the opinions of the lay public, or of the individuals who endow or manage universities.

The members of the faculty of a university are "the appointees, but not in any proper sense the employees," of the governing board.

The responsibility of the university teacher is primarily to the public itself, and to the judgment of his own profession; and while, with respect to certain external conditions of his vocation, he accepts a responsibility to the authorities of the institution in which he serves, in the essentials of his professional activity his duty is to the wider public to which the institution itself is morally amenable.

The relation of the professor to the trustees may be understood upon an analogy with the relation of a judge in a federal court to the Executive who appoints him. Appointed by the President, the judge is expected to render decisions on grounds independent of the President's influence or authority. That manner of freedom is "the breath in the nostrils of all scientific activity." "A university is a great and indispensable organ of the higher life of a civilized community, in the work of which the trustees hold an essential and highly honorable place, but in which the faculties hold an independent place, with quite equal responsibilities—and in relation to purely scientific and educational questions, the primary responsibility."

It is easy to suppose that the *Declaration* is simply an expression of professional piety. It is surely that. Our danger is that we see in it only that. It is in fact the shrewdest insight into the social predicament of the modern professions. The need for recovering this insight appears most forcibly, in the contemporary scene, in the effort of scholars to come to terms with the institution of collective bargaining. Is the movement to constitute the community of scholars a collective bargainer for wages a simple resurrection, in twentieth-century society, of the principles of the twelfth-century guildsman? Is it the bare practice of a *de facto* monopoly? Or is it a mistaken substitution of adherent for inherent obligations, the substitution of a contingent for a privileged beneficiary, in American scholarship?

The American scholar is in process of succumbing to the danger that is implicit in his own historical premises. It is a danger that lies upon all American social institutions at all times, the distrust of our social covenant, the uncritical belief that every positive advance of our society is to be realized out of adversary relations.

The American scholar loves Jefferson; he follows Marshall. Therefore, few are prepared to assess the gravity of the tradition that was resuscitated when, in 1957, the late Justice Felix Frankfurter affirmed "the dependence of free society on free universities."[19] In that opinion the spirit of Thomas Jefferson presided imperiously in John Marshall's Court. For the decision rests on the implied assumption that the freedom of the community of scholars can be justified in one way only, by being shown to be a prerequisite to the increase of freedom elsewhere. The scholar's freedom to investigate and to publish his conclusions is but the correlate of a free society's need to know. Society confers upon him this freedom, not because he asks it, but because what society asks of him requires it. Even in his most solitary and recondite labors he executes a public trust, and what we call his freedom is simply his implied immunity,[20] under the protection of society, to perform those acts which the trust obliges him to perform, which it puts in his care and in its own interest shields from the adventitious interferences of church or state or of other members of the academic community.

4. THE U.S. SUPREME COURT AND THE DELEGATED INTELLECT

Since World War II, in a series of decisions of the Supreme Court, the fiduciary function of scholarship has gained confirmation in the law itself.[21] The justice on the bench has outstripped the scholar at the bargaining table. And it is one of the supreme ironies of our times that the American scholar, "the delegated intellect," at the moment at which the loftiest inherent claims of his profession have been socially recognized, is in danger of forgetting his public commission in pursuit of a private advantage.

The public officer *de facto* is in process of becoming, by judicial acknowledgement, a public officer *de iure*.

In 1892, in a petition for mandamus brought before the Supreme Judicial Court of Massachusetts,[22] the petitioner, one John J. McAuliffe, asked to be reinstated in his former position on the police force of the City of New Bedford. McAuliffe had been dismissed from service for having violated a fixed rule of the police code forbidding any officer to solicit money or aid for political purposes. The petitioner claimed relief on the ground that the rule under which he had been discharged violated his constitutional right to express his political opinions.

Justice Holmes, then on the Massachusetts bench, dismissed the petition:

The petitioner may have a constitutional right to talk politics, but he has no constitutional right to be a policeman. There are few employments for hire in which the servant does not agree to suspend his constitutional rights of free speech as well as of idleness by the implied terms of his contract. The servant cannot complain, as he takes the employment on the terms which are offered him. On the same principle, the city may impose any reasonable condition upon holding offices within its control.

So pregnant of consequence is that simple piece of judicial reasoning that it became the source in American law of a legal doctrine, the doctrine known in the courts as "the doctrine of privilege in public employment."[23] In employing personnel to execute its offices, the public power may set the conditions under which it will consent to be served. The conditions must, as Holmes himself provided, be "reasonable"; they may not be arbitrary or discriminatory.[24] But within these limits the right of the public power to decide what shall and shall not be done by those enlisted in its service is unqualified. The Constitution does not guarantee public employment. No one has an initial right to it. The public employee exercises a privilege. And as the public power confers the privilege, it may also withhold it, on its own terms.

Such is the sense of the doctrine. In 1892 it remained for the courts to determine what restraints might be laid upon employees as reasonable conditions of their public employment. This question excited the most anxious attention among scholars, especially among scholars in public institutions. A scholar who entered public employment needed very much to know whether, under the Constitution, rights of free speech and association that were unabridgeable in the citizen were subject to abridgment, and even to abrogation, in the employee.

This question was squarely confronted, and as summarily disposed of, in the *cause célèbre* of the 1920s, the Scopes trial concerning the teaching of evolution in the public schools of Tennessee. John T. Scopes was convicted and fined $100 for having violated the Tennessee Anti-Evolution Act, an act forbidding any teacher in schools supported by public funds to teach the theory that "man has descended from a lower order of animals."[25] Scopes appealed. The Supreme Court of the State of Tennessee replied:

The plaintiff . . . was an employee of the State of Tennessee or of a municipal agency of the State. He was under contract with the State to work in an institution of the State. He had no right or privilege to serve the State except upon such terms as the State prescribed. His liberty, his privilege, his immunity to teach and proclaim the theory of evolution, elsewhere than in the service of the State, was in no wise touched by this law.

The Statute before us is . . . an Act of the State as a corporation, a proprietor, an employer. It is a declaration of a master as to the character of work the master's servant shall, or rather shall not, perform. In dealing with its own employees engaged upon its own work, the State is not hampered by the limitations . . . of the Fourteenth Amendment of the Constitution of the United States. . . .

In *Adler* v. *Board of Education of the City of New York*[26] the doctrine of privilege in public employment appeared to be clothed with the authority of the Supreme Court of the United States. The matter in contention was the constitutionality of a section of the New York Civil Service Law as it came to be implemented by a statute known as the Feinberg Law. The Feinberg Law required the board of regents to make and maintain a list of organizations that had been found to advocate the violent overthrow of the government. Membership in any listed organization was to constitute *prima facie* evidence for disqualification from service in the public schools of the state. The loyalty program based on these laws was contested on the ground that it violated the due process clause of the Fourteenth Amendment. Justice Minton delivered the opinion of the Court:

It is clear that such persons have the right under our law to assemble, speak, think and believe as they will. . . . It is equally clear that they have no right to work for the State in the school system on their own terms. . . . They work for the school system upon the reasonable terms laid down by the proper authorities of New York. If they do not choose to work on such terms, they are at liberty to retain their beliefs and associations and go elsewhere. Has the State thus deprived them of any right to free speech or assembly? We think not. Such persons are or may be denied, under the statutes in question, the privilege of working for the school system of the State of New York.

In this instance, however, in a dissenting opinion, the doctrine of privilege was directly challenged. Justice Douglas removed himself from the decision of the Court with one of the memorable pronouncements in the literature of dissent. His opinion is the first explicit acknowledgment, at the level of our highest tribunal, of *academic freedom as a condition of free society*. The exercise of the free intellect is apprehended as an obligation that falls, not exclusively upon the teacher, but surely upon him, and by virtue of his function in society more exigently upon him than upon others. Justice Douglas wrote:

I have not been able to accept the recent doctrine that a citizen who enters the public service can be forced to sacrifice his civil rights. . . . The Constitution guarantees freedom of thought and expression to everyone in our society. All are entitled to it; and none needs it more than the teacher.

The public school is in most respects the cradle of our democracy. The increasing role of the public school is seized upon . . . as proof of the importance and need for keeping the school free of "subversive influences." But that is to misconceive the effect of this type of legislation. . . .

What happens under this law is typical of what happens in a police state. . . . A pall is cast over the classrooms. There can be no real academic freedom in that environment. Where suspicion fills the air and holds scholars in line for fear of their jobs, there can be no exercise of the free intellect. Supineness and dogmatism take the place of inquiry. A "party line" . . . lays hold. It is the "party line" of the orthodox view, of the conventional thought, of the accepted approach. A problem can no longer be pursued with impunity to its edges. . . . A deadening dogma takes the place of free inquiry. Instruction tends to become sterile; pursuit of knowledge is discouraged; discussion often leaves off where it should begin.

. . . This system of spying and surveillance . . . cannot go hand in hand with academic freedom. It produces standardized thought, not the pursuit of truth. Yet it was the pursuit of truth which the First Amendment was designed to protect.

That opinion, when it was written, was the the dissent of a minority.[27] It has since become, in a succession of important decisions, the confirmed position of the Court. The effect of these decisions is to declare the constitutional limitations that hedge the use of the doctrine of privilege in public employment. Public employment (such is the judgment of the Court) may not be made to rest on an arbitrary suspension of the conditions of ordinary freedom. The rights guaranteed in the Constitution—rights of free speech and expression, rights of assembly and association, rights of due process and equality before the law—are necessary to our form of society, and no condition of employment that arbitrarily abridges them will, in the contemplation of the Court, be accounted reasonable under the law.

I am able to cite only a very narrow sampling of these decisions. The matter that interests us in them is the matter that interested Douglas, not the praise of scholars, not the celebration of the community of scholars as a sufficient good, but *the firm conception of scholarship as a public commission*. The effect of these decisions is to recognize, in the formal development of the law itself, the fiduciary function of free scholarship in American society.

"Of course," says Justice Harlan, speaking for the Court in *Barenblatt* v. *United States*,[28] "broadly viewed, inquiries cannot be made into the teaching that is pursued in any of our educational institutions. When academic teaching-freedom and its corollary learning-freedom, so essential to the well-being of the Nation, are claimed, this Court will always be on the alert against intrusion by Congress into this constitutionally protected domain." The free scholar performs an autonomous public commission upon which even the legislature is forbidden to trespass unless, in the judgment of the Court itself, overriding obligations of the public safety clearly require it. The exercise of the free intellect in institutions of teaching and learning has become, in judicial interpretation, a corporate undertaking no longer merely private. In legal status as in social function, it implicates the public interest. It is a "constitutionally protected domain."[29]

The Court nevertheless upheld Barenblatt's conviction for contempt of Congress for refusing to answer questions put to him by the House Committee on Un-American Activities. When First Amendment protection is claimed, wrote Harlan,[30] the resolution always involves "a balancing by the courts of the competing private and public interests at stake in the particular circumstances shown." The balance in the case at hand was struck in favor of the governmental interest. Justice Hugo L. Black (joined by Chief Justice Warren and Justice Douglas) dissented:[31]

I do not agree that laws directly abridging First Amendment freedoms can be justified by a congressional or judicial balancing process. . . .

Unless . . . we once again accept the notion that the Bill of Rights means what it says and that this Court must enforce that meaning, . . . our great charter of liberty will be more honored in the breach than in the observance. . . .

It is this right, the right to err politically, which keeps us strong as a Nation. For no number of laws against communism can have as much effect as the personal conviction which comes from having heard its arguments and rejected them, or from having once accepted its tenets and later recognized their worthlessness. . . . This result . . . is doubly crucial when it affects the universities. . . .

. . . the only constitutional way our Government can preserve itself is to leave its people the fullest possible freedom to praise, criticize or discuss, as they see fit, all governmental policies and to suggest, if they desire, that even its most fundamental postulates are bad and should be changed. . . .

Ultimately all the questions in this case really boil down to one— . . . whether in accordance with our tradition and our Constitution we will have the confidence and courage to be free.

In 1952, in *Wieman* v. *Updegraff*,[32] the Supreme Court struck down an Oklahoma statute requiring loyalty oaths of state employees. Since the action proceeded from a refusal of teachers at Oklahoma Agricultural and Mechanical College to take the oath, Justice Frankfurter chose to expatiate at length on "the functions of educational institutions in our national life." He wrote:

That our democracy ultimately rests on public opinion is a platitude of speech but not a commonplace in action. Public opinion is the ultimate reliance of our society only if it be disciplined and responsible. It can be disciplined and responsible only if habits of open-mindedness and of critical inquiry are acquired in the formative years of our citizens. . . .

To regard teachers—in our entire educational system, from the primary grades to the university—as the priests of our democracy is therefore not to indulge in hyperbole. It is the special task of teachers to foster those habits of open-mindedness and critical inquiry which alone make for responsible citizens. . . . They must have the freedom of responsible inquiry, by thought and action, into the meaning of social and economic ideas, into the checkered history of social and economic dogma. They must be free to sift evanescent doctrine, qualified by time and circumstance, from that restless, enduring process of extending the bounds of understanding and wisdom, to assure which the freedoms of thought, of speech, of inquiry, of worship are guaranteed by the Constitution of the United States against infraction by national or state government.

In 1951 the legislature of New Hampshire passed a statute, the New Hampshire Subversive Activities Act, designed to eliminate such activities from the agencies of government and from public educational institutions. A supplementary resolution authorized the attorney general to act as a one-man legislative committee, exercising the legislature's investigative powers, in order to prepare the way for criminal prosecutions under the act.

Paul M. Sweezy, an editor, was summoned to appear before the attorney general. By invitation of members of the faculty of the University of New Hampshire, Sweezy had delivered a lecture on socialism to a class of one hundred students. Sweezy described himself as a "classical Marxist" and a "socialist"; he denied that he had ever been a member of the Communist party or of any movement that sought the overthrow of the government by force or violence. However, in a prepared statement, he declined to answer questions that were not pertinent to the inquiry or that transgressed his rights under the First Amendment. He refused to disclose his knowledge of the Progressive party, the party of former Vice President Henry A. Wallace, in the 1948 presidential election. (On the ballot in forty-four states including New Hampshire, the Progressive party had received 1,156,103 votes in the nation, 1,970 votes in the state of New Hampshire.) More particularly, Sweezy declined to answer questions concerning the content of the lecture. The attorney general, since he was not empowered to hold witnesses in contempt, petitioned the superior court to propose the same questions. When Sweezy, in the face of the court's ruling that the questions were pertinent, persisted in his refusal to answer, the court ordered him committed to the county jail until purged of its citation of contempt. The New Hampshire Supreme Court affirmed the lower court's decision. The judgment was reversed in the Supreme Court of the United States in *Sweezy* v. *New Hampshire.*[33]

"There is no doubt," said Chief Justice Warren in announcing the judgment of the Court,[34] "that legislative investigations, whether on a federal or state level, are capable of encroaching upon the constitutional liberties of individuals. It is particularly important that the exercise of the power of com-

pulsory process be carefully circumscribed when the investigative process tends to impinge upon such highly sensitive
areas as freedom of speech or press, freedom of political association, and freedom of communication of ideas, particularly
in the academic community."

We believe that there unquestionably was an invasion of petitioner's
liberties in the areas of academic freedom and political expression—
areas in which government should be extremely reticent to tread.

The essentiality of freedom in the community of American universities is almost self-evident. No one should underestimate the vital role
in a democracy that is played by those who guide and train our
youth. To impose any strait jacket upon the intellectual leaders in our
colleges and universitites would imperil the future of our Nation.
. . . Scholarship cannot flourish in an atmosphere of suspicion and
distrust. Teachers and students must always remain free to inquire,
to study and to evaluate, to gain new maturity and understanding;
otherwise our civilization will stagnate and die. . . .

Mere unorthodoxy or dissent from the prevailing mores is not to be
condemned. The absence of such voices would be a symptom of
grave illness in our society.[35]

This decision does not in fact confer an unqualified immunity on the pronouncements of scholars. The Court is
obliged, in judging the actions of scholars as in judging the
actions of other citizens, to balance "two contending principles"[36]—the right of the individual to political privacy and the
right of the state to self-protection. But the work of the scholar,
when the scholar works in his fiduciary capacity, is not, as the
Court views it, a merely private commission. It is a public
commission, essential (even when it offends against established opinions concerning the public interest) for discovering
where in fact, if the public were fully informed, the public
interest would be held to lie.

Democracy is not a composition of men's ignorance; it is
the affirmation that an informed public knows what it wants
and is content to accept the risks of learning, even the critical
risk of learning that what it wants is not always what it
thought it wanted. To supply the resources of criticism in a

free society is the public function of scholarship; the university is its institutional correlate.

"Political power," wrote Justice Frankfurter, "must abstain from intrusion into this activity of freedom, pursued in the interest of wise government and the people's well-being, except for reasons that are exigent and obviously compelling."

These pages need not be burdened with proof, based on the testimony of a cloud of impressive witnesses, of the dependence of a free society on free universities. . . . Suffice it to quote the latest expression on this subject. . . .

". . . the spirit of free inquiry . . . implies the right to examine, question, modify or reject traditional ideas and beliefs. Dogma and hypothesis are incompatible, and the concept of an immutable doctrine is repugnant to the spirit of a university. The concern of its scholars is not merely to add and revise facts in relation to an accepted framework, but to be ever examining and modifying the framework itself. . . .

"It is the business of a university to provide . . . an atmosphere in which there prevail 'the four essential freedoms' of a university—to determine for itself on academic grounds who may teach, what may be taught, how it shall be taught, and who may be admitted to study."[37]

The university is not, and may never claim to be, a sanctuary from the law; it is nevertheless beneath the shelter of the law, the delegated argument of a free society with itself. The public argument must be held permanently in the public domain, and the scholar is by implied power, *de iure*, its burdened public officer.

NOTES

1. The demand for a clear delegation of authority is the ground for the insistence on the consent of the patient, which recurs with perfect regularity in all modern codes for clinical investigation. "The investigator," says Beecher's Code (1966) with curt decisiveness, "has no right to choose martyrs for science." The first principle of the Nuremberg Code (1946–1949) declares: "The voluntary consent of the human subject is absolutely essential. This means that the person in-

volved should have legal capacity to consent; should be so situated as to be able to exercise free power of choice, without the intervention of any element of force, fraud, deceit, duress, overreaching, or other ulterior form of constraint or coercion; and should have sufficient knowledge and comprehension of the elements of the subject matter involved as to enable him to make an understanding and enlightened decision."

The Declaration of Geneva of the World Medical Association (1964) binds the doctor with the oath: "The health of my patient will be my first consideration."

The Declaration of Helsinki (1962, revised 1964) recognizes the difficulties of obtaining an informed consent from children, ignorant persons, or those who are mentally unsound, confused, unconscious or anaesthetized; it nevertheless lays down the principles: "Clinical research on a human being cannot be undertaken without his free consent, after he has been fully informed; if he is legally incompetent the consent of the legal guardian should be procured. . . . At any time during the course of clinical research the subject or his guardian should be free to withdraw permission for research to be continued."

2. Cf. Theodore Caplow and Reece J. McGee, *The Academic Marketplace* (New York: Basic Books, 1958).

3. Hippocrates, *Works, with an English Translation by W. H. S. Jones*, Loeb Classical Library (New York: G. P. Putnam, 1923), vol. I, "Precept vi," p. 319. Cf. "The Canons of Professional Ethics of the American Bar Association" (Chicago: Martindale-Hubbell, [1959?]), p. 6, Canon 12: "A client's ability to pay cannot justify a charge in excess of the value of the service, though his poverty may require a less charge, or even none at all."

4. "The Prayer of Moses Maimonides," in M. B. Etziony, *The Physician's Creed* (Springfield, Ill.: Charles C. Thomas, 1973), pp. 29–30.

5. Andrew Dickson White, *Autobiography* (New York: Century, 1905), vol. I, p. 336.

6. *The Federalist*, No. 79.

7. *On Liberty*, ii.

8. Hastings Rashdall, *The Universities of Europe in the Middle Ages*, edited by F. M. Powicke and A. B. Emden (Oxford: Clarendon Press, 1895), vol. I, pp. 150–160, at p. 150.

9. J. K. Hyde, "Early Medieval Bologna," in *Universities in Politics, Case Studies from the Late Middle Ages and Early Modern Period*, edited by John W. Baldwin and Richard A. Goldthwaite (Baltimore: The Johns Hopkins University Press, 1972), pp. 32–33: "Scholars living outside their native city . . . might be held responsible for the

debts of their fellow citizens, whether students, merchants, or others, by the authorities of the city in which they were studying."

10. Rashdall, op. cit., vol. I, pp. 290–292 and 291, n. 1.

11. Jefferson to William Roscoe, December 27, 1820, in *The Writings of Thomas Jefferson*, edited by Andrew A. Lipscomb (Washington, D.C.: The Thomas Jefferson Memorial Association, 1904), vol. XV, p. 303. Hereafter referred to as the *Library Edition*.

12. Ibid. Jefferson is drawing from his own First Inaugural Address (March 4, 1801): "Error of opinion may be tolerated where reason is left free to combat it." *Library Edition*, vol. III, p. 319.

13. *As You Like It*, II, vii.

14. Jefferson to William C. Jarvis, September 28, 1820, in *Library Edition*, vol. XV, p. 378.

15. Quoted by George E. Baker, "Thomas Jefferson on Academic Freedom," 39 *AAUP Bulletin* (1953): 384, n. 1.

16. Jefferson to George Ticknor, July 16, 1823, in *Library Edition*, vol. XV, p. 457.

17. *The Trustees of Dartmouth College* v. *Woodward*, 4 Wheaton 625–654 (1819). The quotations below occur, respectively, at 634 and 641.

18. 40 *AAUP Bulletin* (1954): 89–112. It is not known by whom the *Declaration* was written, but the traditional presumption has been that the drafting author was either the chairman, E. R. A. Seligman, or Arthur Lovejoy, who was at the same time serving as the association's first secretary. Lovejoy was at all events the author of the most generally quoted definition of academic freedom. It appears in his article, "Academic Freedom," in *Encyclopaedia of the Social Sciences* (1930), vol. I, p. 384. "Academic freedom is the freedom of the teacher or research worker in higher institutions of learning to investigate and discuss the problems of his science and to express his conclusions, whether through publication or in the instruction of students, without interference from political or ecclesiastical authority, or from the administrative officials of the institution in which he is employed, unless his methods are found by qualified bodies of his own profession to be clearly incompetent or contrary to professional ethics."

19. *Sweezy* v. *New Hampshire*, 354 U.S. 234, 262 (1957). Cf. the opinion of Mr. Justice Brennan in *Keyishian* v. *Board of Regents*, 385 U.S. 589, 603, (1967): "Academic freedom . . . is of transcendent value to all of us and not merely to the teachers concerned."

Justice Frankfurter was himself perfectly aware of the tradition in which he spoke. Cf. *Wieman* v. *Updegraff*, 344 U.S. 183, 196 (1952): "Public opinion is the ultimate reliance of our society only if it be disciplined and responsible. . . . The process of education has naturally enough been the basis of hope for the perdurance of our democracy on the part of all our great leaders, from Thomas Jefferson onwards."

20. William W. Van Alstyne construes academic freedom as a "liberty," that is, as "an immunity from the power of others," rather than a "right." Cf. "The Specific Theory of Academic Freedom and the General Issue of Civil Liberties," 404 *Annals of the American Academy of Political and Social Science* (1972): 140, 146–147.

21. Cf. William P. Murphy, "Academic Freedom—An Emerging Constitutional Right," in *Academic Freedom, The Scholar's Place in Modern Society*, edited by Hans W. Baade and Robinson O. Everett (Dobbs Ferry, N.Y.: Oceana Publications, 1964), pp. 17–56. This article—without question the finest brief compendium in the literature—appears in a different version, under the title "Educational Freedom in the Courts," in 49 *AAUP Bulletin* (1963). 309–327. See also "Developments in the Law—Academic Freedom," 81 *Harvard Law Review* (1968): 1045–1159.

22. *McAuliffe* v. *Mayor of the City of New Bedford*, 155 Mass. 216, 220; 29 N.E. 517, 518 (1892).

23. Cf. Arch Dotson, "The Emerging Doctrine of Privilege in Public Employment," 15 *Public Administration Review* (1955): 77–88. The doctrine is restricted to public employments only.

24. *Wieman* v. *Updegraff*, 344 U.S. 183, 191–192 (1952). Justice Clark, speaking for the Court, stated: "In *United Public Workers*, though we held that the federal government through the Hatch Act could properly bar its employees from certain types of political activity thought inimical to the interests of the Civil Service, we cast this holding into perspective by emphasizing that Congress could not 'enact a regulation providing that no Republican, Jew or Negro shall be appointed to federal office, or that no federal employee shall attend Mass or take any active part in missionary work.' . . . We need not pause to consider whether an abstract right to public employment exists. It is sufficient to say that constitutional protection does extend to the public servant whose exclusion pursuant to a statute is patently arbitrary or discriminatory."

25. *Scopes* v. *State*, 154 Tenn. 105, 111; 289 S.W. 363, 364 (1927).

26. *Adler* v. *Board of Education of the City of New York*, 342 U.S. 485 (1952). The quotations occur, respectively, at 492 and at 508–511.

27. Justice Black concurred in the opinion. Justice Frankfurter, who wrote a separate dissenting opinion, nevertheless took the occasion to confirm the posture as his own. Freedom of thought, inquiry, and expression are "part of the necessary professional equip-

ment of teachers in a free society" (id. at 504–505). Frankfurter had already declared himself in *Garner* v. *Board of Public Works of City of Los Angeles*, 34 U.S. 716, 724–725 (1951): "The Constitution does not guarantee public employment. . . . But it does not at all follow that because the Constitution does not guarantee a right to public employment, a city or a state may resort to any scheme for keeping people out of such employment. . . . unreasonable discriminations, if avowed in formal law, would not survive constitutional challenge. . . . To describe public employment as a privilege does not meet the problem."

28. 360 U.S. 109, 112 (1959).

29. The "protected domain" does not make of the university a sanctuary from the law. The passage quoted is followed at once by the sentences: "But this does not mean that the Congress is precluded from interrogating a witness merely because he is a teacher. An educational institution is not a constitutional sanctuary from inquiry into matters that may otherwise be within the constitutional legislative domain merely for the reason that inquiry is made of someone within its walls."

30. Ibid., 126.

31. Ibid., 141, 143–144, 146, 162.

32. 344 U.S. 183, 196–197 (1952).

33. 354 U.S. 234 (1956).

34. Ibid., 245. There was no majority decision. Justices Black, Douglas, and Brennan joined in the opinion of the Chief Justice. Justice Frankfurter wrote a separate concurring opinion in which he was joined by Justice Harlan.

35. Ibid., 250–251.

36. Ibid., 266 (Frankfurter).

37. Ibid., 262–263. The quotation is from a statement of a conference of senior scholars from the University of Cape Town and the University of Witwatersrand, including their respective chancellors, the then recently retired Chief Justice of South Africa, A. v. d. S. Centlivres, and Richard Feetham, a retired South African judge.

4.

THE FOURTH BRANCH
OF GOVERNMENT

1. THE CUSTODY OF COMMONWEALTH

When in the political ordering of our affairs we distribute the legislative, the executive, and the judicial powers of government into different hands, it must appear to any external observer, to any observer not implicated in our political process, that we behave most irrationally. We separate functions that are in fact complementary, and it is evident that for purposes of efficiency the separation of complementary functions is of all possible arrangements the most complicated and the worst.

For ourselves, however, who view the life of our society as parties to it from within, efficiency is not of course the motive. Our motive in separating the powers of government is not to advance the interests of our society against the world; our motive is to defend the security of our society against ourselves. The separation of powers has but one object, to make dishonesty inconvenient. The ancient philosophers used to

despair over the question, *Quis custodiet ipsos custodes?*—
"Who shall guard the guardians?" If guardians are needed to
keep watch over us, shall no guardian be needed to keep
watch over them? The American Constitution resolves the
problem by forestalling it. By sovereign cunning it sets the
guardians to watching each other in a system of calculated
checks and balances. The system generates honesty even
where no one is willing to assume it. Or, more accurately, it
eliminates dishonesty even where everyone is predisposed to
expect it. By playing the gravitating elements of an arch
against each other, an engineer employs the very forces that
would destroy the arch for the purpose of holding it aloft. In
government we employ the same device.

Years ago, when I first began to reflect upon the political
relations of the university in contemporary life, the idea that
the scientific community was in process of becoming, in fact
if not in law, a fourth branch of government, was very disturbing to me. For the question at once arose, not whether the
scientific community commanded the resources essential to a
branch of government, but what check it was to have, what
check would be consistent with its necessary autonomy.

Mr. William F. Buckley, Jr., once acidulously declared that
he would sooner be governed by the first two thousand names
in the Boston telephone directory than by the two thousand
members of the faculty of Harvard University. In candor I
must admit to sharing this opinion, if not its irreverence for
intellect, at all events its frank approval of the Irish. There is
nevertheless in Mr. Buckley's opinion an element of illusion.
It is one of the extraordinary ironies of contemporary history
that to be governed by the first two thousand names in the
Boston telephone directory is nowadays in fact, transitively, to
be governed by the Harvard faculty. If the modern university
is not the rod, it has certainly become the staff of the commonwealth. And I know nothing that so accurately reflects the
modern transformation as those lines which John Maynard
Keynes wrote at the conclusion of his *General Theory of Employment, Interest and Money:*

The ideas of economists and political philosophers, both when they are right and when they are wrong, are more powerful than is commonly understood. Indeed the world is ruled by little else. Practical men, who believe themselves to be quite exempt from any intellectual influences, are usually the slaves of some defunct economist. Madmen in authority, who hear voices in the air, are distilling their frenzy from some academic scribbler of a few years back. . . . soon or late, it is ideas, not vested interests, which are dangerous for good or evil.[1]

Keynes knew, if his contemporaries did not, that thought is indivorcible from act, that every belief is an implicit advocacy, whose meaning must be understod, if it would be understood at all, in practice. No one in those days ever dreamed of "politicizing" the university, and when a madman in authority actually did it, did it with a German thoroughness, no one doubted that the consequences were so manifest and regrettable as never to be repeated by the sane. The custom was, in those days, to mark a firm distinction between the world, the flesh, and the devil on the one side and the academy on the other. And it was part of the game played by all academics to show that if the devil walked in the world, then he could not walk in the academy, since, as everybody knew, the academy was out of the world. The distinction, it must be admitted, was not drawn exactly in those terms. The terms were older and more recondite. They relied upon the difference that Aristotle supposed himself to find between the theoretical and the practical employment of reason, between reason as a speculative and reason as a deliberative faculty. That distinction is so firmly entrenched in habit that it is almost impossible, except by felicity of illustration, to dislodge it. That is why Keynes' lines are treasurable, and why as a young man I used to place beside them a dissenting opinion of Mr. Justice Holmes:

Every idea is an incitement. It offers itself for belief, and, if believed, it is acted on unless some other belief outweighs it. . . .[2]

Those simple sentences convey a very fundamental text of political theory. For if indeed it is true that every idea is acted on in the measure that it is believed, it must then follow that the control of a man's beliefs is the most direct path to the control of his actions. Give to another the power to govern your beliefs, he has all the power that he shall ever need to govern you. You will die for a falsehood you believe more willingly than live for a truth you repudiate, and if for a belief you hold true you be denied that vision of alternatives that would enable you to doubt it or to prove it false, you will endure in dumb innocence what would revolt you in clear knowledge. That sinister perception lies at the foundation of every effective tyranny in the history of the world. But it lies also at the foundation of any understanding of the role the university is called upon to enact in the free world. The function of criticism, of open discussion, of inquiry and argument, by which beliefs are winnowed, is an indispensable condition of free society, as indispensable for our political process as a legislature, or as an executive, or as a judiciary.

Forty years ago the idea of a university beyond politics was a supportable description of its actual behavior. Scholars might imagine the uses of the university as a reservoir of intellectual power in the national life; a new political leader, to meet a national emergency, might summon a "brain trust" to his side. But in the public understanding the primary function of the university was education—not science, not research, not invention or discovery, but the cultivation of the young and the training of professionals. The experience of two generations has changed that. The marriage of science and government in America since World War II is one of the great new facts of American life; it touches the constitution of our society and promises to become, before the century has run its course, one of the most vexed and problematic relations of American politics.

2. SCIENCE AND GOVERNMENT

George Washington recommended to his countrymen the establishment of a national university. So firmly persuaded was our first president that "a flourishing state of the Arts and Sciences contributes to National prosperity and reputation" that he left a bequest to the nation for this purpose. "True it is," said Washington in his last address to Congress in 1796, "that our Country, much to its honor, contains many Seminaries of learning highly respectable and useful; but the funds upon which they rest are too narrow to command the ablest Professors, in the different departments of liberal knowledge, for the institution contemplated." The existing seminaries would be "excellent auxiliaries" to the recommended national establishment, but they could not substitute for it.[3]

Washington's recommendation, which was repeated by the next five presidents in succession, produced no issue, and the bequest went unused. Congress chose rather to rely on the "excellent auxiliaries." It still does. The establishment of the public university was left to the states; the establishment of the private university, to foundations and endowments. Congress found in the federal grant and the putting out of contracts a path more suited to the pluralist premises of the new republic. But this path, though it is in principle profoundly obedient to the national character, has led in the last quarter century to a result totally unpremeditated—not to a decentralization of the control of science by the federal government, but to the abrogation of the direct control of science by any government.

The typical nineteenth-century pattern of administering the work of science in the public interest is the pattern of the Morrill Act of 1862. The land-grant institutions were created out of the public domain. They were the product of a general charter, the administration of which was left, in the detail of its execution, to its beneficiaries, that is, to the states. Within the terms of the charter the states were to define their own interests and to establish such institutions of useful learning as would contribute to their advancement. The Hatch Act of 1887, which established the American system of agricultural experiment stations, was an extension of the same principle. Annual appropriations supplied the resources of experiment;

the direction of experiment was expressly reserved to the colleges and to their departments on the assumption that the local agencies were better equipped than the federal government to judge of local needs and to respond to them. The institutions remained accountable; their projects required coordination and approval; but the approving agencies of the government were forbidden to appropriate to themselves the initiatives that belonged, by declaration of Congress, to the local centers.

The pattern that has evolved in the twentieth century is based on a different principle. It relies not on a general charter to the states but on specific contracts with their agencies, with private institutions, and even with individuals. Its principle is *the clientism of government.*

The new strategy of administering the progress of science directly in the public interest was discovered in the example of the great foundations instituted by private philanthropy at the beginning of the century. Carnegie, Rockefeller, and (at midcentury) Ford were in fact the seeds of a new birth in the face of the land. John Marshall would have described them, as he described little Dartmouth, as "eleemosynary institutions"—private, propertied, donative of charity. But there was this difference, that the foundations were by conception general-purpose institutions. The beneficiaries of their munificence were not this or that special class of individuals, not Indians or frontiersmen, but the primary institutions of society itself, hospitals and charities, schools and libraries, all of the beneficial institutions, public or private, out of which direct social effects flow. The primary institutions of a society distribute their benefits directly to the people—the hospital to the patient, the charity to the indigent, the school and the library to the student. Therefore, to influence these institutions—not the student but the pattern of education, not the patient but the quality and distribution of hospital services— is indirectly to influence, in the most intimate and strategically powerful connections, the lives of men.

The great private foundations take this as their public commission. General-purpose institutions, they produce social change by indirection, affecting institutions first and individuals only through them. Great looseners of the social arrest of our primary institutions, they are part of the organizational revolution of our time. If they transcend the limits of seminaries as ordinarily conceived, they do so because they are designed, like government, to work at the administration of scholarship at a second remove. They do by indirection for society at large what the seminaries did, locally and parochially, for the student beneficiaries who came under their special care. The Carnegie Institute of Washington encourages "the application of knowledge to the improvement of mankind"; the Carnegie Corporation of New York aims at "the advancement and diffusion of knowledge and understanding" among the people. The charter of the Ford Foundation embraces the same unspecialized commission, "to receive and administer funds for scientific, educational, and charitable purposes, all for the public welfare." The aims vary in detail, but in all of them occurs the same emphasis on the centrality of science in the public life. "All important fields of activity, from the breeding of bees to the administration of an empire," said Rockefeller's Wickliffe Rose, "call for an understanding of the spirit and technique of modern science. . . . Science is the key to such dominion as man may ever exercise over his physical environment. Appreciation of its spirit and technique . . . determines the mental attitude of a people, affects the entire system of education, and carries with it the shaping of a civilization."[4]

Let then this spirit and technique be diffused through all the avenues of human intercourse, let it be brought to bear upon institutions, the simplest and the grandest, that men live by, it will transform civilizations, establishments, manners, the idea of education, and the conditions of public health, like giant Mississippi, impatient of its ancient bed, which overwhelms its banks, sweeps artificial dikes before it, and carves straighter corridors to the sea.

The modern foundations are the corporate modern version of the wandering scholar. Formerly, the scholar wandered;

now, the foundation wanders and the scholar (at least occasionally) stays at home. The foundation reaches into the local institution, attracts expertise to the projects it is willing to sponsor, enables society to rise above the fortuitous accidents by which, historically, disciplined powers were addressed to the needs of society. Of all of society's private institutions the foundations labor most consciously in the clear awareness of the essential placelessness of the scientific establishment. The establishment is not in Massachusetts or Maryland, not in California or Illinois; it is wherever the scholar practices his great surmise, wherever eminent talent has been conjoined, beyond place, with the spirit and technique of modern science.

The foundations perceived the relation of the higher learning to social change. They discovered the intimation of the power of science as an internally autonomous structure, capable by policy of being activated in directions that statesmanship, private of public, has elected.

In this accession of support the scholar, who is their agent of change, has gone silently about his labors without obliging himself to reflect on the great transformations he is party to. Answerable only to his professional colleagues, to panels of experts who are capable of judging his technical performance, he is, like the ancient guildsman, active in the employment but passive in the system. The institution of scholarship is not a hierarchical structure; the private foundation that employs scholars is precisely that. And it was prepared to demonstrate that, under right direction, an informed gathering of the critical powers of our society would serve to liberate all of our other powers.

The rightness of the direction was, however, a matter of gravest .solicitude, and Congress viewed the foundations, in spite of their manifest benefactions, with a jaundiced eye. "Should we permit a segment of our society to set up a government of its own to render philanthropic services?" The question, put by an irate Republican congressman to the House Ways and Means Committee in hearings on tax reform, was by no means impertinent.[5] Existing legislation permitted, for charitable purposes, an unlimited deduction from taxable income. Therefore, when the hearings for the Tax Reform Act of 1969 produced the revelation that John D. Rockefeller III had paid no income tax for the last eight years in succession, the legislators responded in ways suited to the strained public temper of the season. It was unnecessary to impute to the donor of charity a malicious neglect of public duty. Congress believed that its prerogatives had been invaded. The private omission intruded upon its public authority, and in reprehending the offense it refused to consider the public spirit that may have animated the giver of largesse. "Our tax laws," said the congressman, "give one group a chance to . . . make their own determination as to what is in the public good."[6] The determination of the public good belonged to the people's representatives, and when wealth was employed, even in demonstrably constructive and disinterested public uses, to shape civilization, Congress was unwilling to renounce its privilege. It was one thing under private auspices to eradicate the baneful effects of hookworm in the South; it was another to permit a concentration of private wealth to extend its influence to race relations and voter registration, in which public opinion was formed, in the same site. The body politic was, in the estimation of Congress, perfectly well equipped to function without an artificial heart. Traditions of academic freedom were supportable in the disheveled anarchy of opinion of an academic faculty; they were intolerable in a foundation that was licensed to wield the scalpel of criticism with the precision of a surgeon. Effectively, on sensitive issues of social welfare—education and noncommercial television, public health and urban development, environmental protection and energy conservation, civil rights and population control—Congress claimed to itself its ancient authority and was as indisposed to elevate the private foundation as it was indisposed to elevate the private industrial corporation to a place above the law.

However, what was reprovable in the private person was admissible in the public, and Congress, though it rejected the invasion of its office, did not hesitate to adopt the techniques of the invader. Since the end of World War II it has turned systematically to the universities, to the same "excellent auxiliaries" upon which the private foundations drew, and proceeded to retain the services of the ablest professors of the higher learning in foundations of its own. By formal acts of legislation, in the establishment of the National Science Foundation and the National Endowment for the Humanities, the law has been made to declare the public office of a scholarship that the society was already, under private auspices, actively affirming.[7]

In 1944, in a letter addressed to Vannevar Bush, Franklin Delano Roosevelt placed before the Office of Scientific Research and Development the problem of the relation of science and government in the future peace. The President asked to be informed what the government could do by way of continuing to aid scientific research when the war ended. "New frontiers of the mind are before us," he wrote, "and if they are pioneered with the same vision, boldness, and drive with which we have waged this war we can create a fuller and more fruitful employment and a fuller and more fruitful life." Bush responded to the President in a report entitled *Science, the Endless Frontier*.[8] He proposed, in effect, the establishment of a national foundation for research in the basic sciences. The report proceeded from a premise which Roosevelt was fully prepared to accept. In a society founded on technology, science is the initial form of capital, the initial form that capital takes under modern conditions of peace and war. Basic research is therefore essential to the public interest, not because it conduces to the illimitable freedom of the human mind, but because it has become a necessity in the life of nations. Never again must our nation be obliged, in time of emergency and public peril, to borrow its fundamental science from abroad. The nation must maintain in seasons of tranquility the scientific preeminence it has achieved in seasons of war. Therefore, Bush argued, it is an indispensable requirement of the national interest that universities and endowed research institutes—the public and private agencies that tradition has qualified, and competence equipped, to perform the tasks of basic science—be strengthened by the use of public funds. The delicate problem politically, as Bush saw even then, was not how to get money but how to use it, how to provide a continuous support for basic research without compromising the independence of the scientific community that was to perform it.

The legislation creating the National Science Foundation was enacted in 1950. No single dispensation of government has so directly implicated the university in the effective processes of our society; none has created so permanent a threat to the public understanding of its detached commission, or rendered it so liable to the political stresses that run in American society against government itself. For it destroyed at one stroke the distinction between the public and the private university. Functionally, if one views the modern university in the terms of its real relationships, the distinction between the private and the public university is without interest in our society.

Carl Kaysen has written of the universities during the years since World War II that "the new central importance of science and scholarship" has rested on a foundation of federal money and is threatened as that support is weakened or withdrawn.[9] The actual magnitude of the transformation surpasses the imagination even of the agencies that are party to it. Dean D. K. Price has written:

No major university today could carry on its research program without federal money. The Massachusetts Institute of Technology, California Institute of Technology, Chicago, and Johns Hopkins . . . all administer special military or atomic energy programs and consequently draw from three fifths to five sixths of their budgets from government. Harvard, Yale, and Princeton now [1960–61] get a larger proportion of their operating revenues from federal funds than do land-grant colleges like Illinois, Iowa State, and North Carolina.[10]

"By 1968," says the Carnegie Commission on Higher Education in a report published in 1971, "about three-fourths of all university research was federally financed."[11] This description makes no distinction between private and public universities.

It makes no distinction for the simple reason that in the new relation of science and government nothing depends on that distinction. By 1968 the federal government had learned, in the phrasing of Mr. Price, "how to socialize without assuming ownership."[12] The ritual distinctions of property remain in fact undisturbed. But the real relations have altered. The effective relations run between professionals—between scientific professionals in government and scientific professionals out of it. The professionals, letting contracts and receiving them, come and go collegially with a frequency measured indeed by the public purse but with an independence measured only by their peers. The federal government may grant support or withhold it; but it is not competent to govern its commissioners or to perform or police their critical offices. All modern governments are related to the scientific community as a patient is related to his medical physician, or a litigant to his lawyer, or a bridgebuilder to his engineer—not by understanding but by clientism. Congress has socialized the process without socializing the scientist. And it can no longer postpone the constitutional problem of having erected a statutory agency to a place in the commonwealth coordinate with its own.

3. THE CLIENTISM OF GOVERNMENT IN ITS OWN DOMAIN

A scholar in the faculty of an American university has no freedom as a professor which he has not already as a citizen; but he has obligations as a professor which the ordinary citizen dreams not of. Economically, as an outsider sees him, he is the employee of a corporation that buys his services. Professionally, as he sees himself, he is the member of an intellectual commonwealth, allied with other scholars in a community of learning that extends beyond his university, beyond his nation, beyond his generation or his time. In that extended historical community he holds himself, even in the absence of external constraints, subject to the discipline of a self-imposed rule. He consents to the norm of the professional community

as to an obligation which he has laid freely on himself. Not
that he does not, on occasion, err against it. Err he may, and
sometimes does; but he is aware of his own offense even before another protests against it, and even when no other
knows to protest. He views his performance—the simplest
confirmation of a matter of fact, the most elementary proof of
a theorem—as *objectively criticizable,* that is, as amenable to a
professional judgment, which determines its rightness according to a standard that is independent of his private interest,
predilection, or advantage.[13]

We have therefore in scholarship an illustration of the
general truth, that the standard of a professional is set, not by
the client who retains his services, but by the professional
community that certifies his privilege, and is capable also of
rescinding his privilege, independently of the client's satisfaction or indifference or disgust.

The structure of professional service implies a divorce of
technical control from direct accountability to the person
served. Where professional and client have no other social
bond, wherever they admit no moral or political covenant that
transcends their inequality in technical intercourse, the professional stands in fact, with respect to the client who retains
him, *in loco parentis.* The lay public is always at the mercy of
the professional for the reason that it is never prepared, except
by his offices, to judge the quality of the services it receives.
The paradox is familiar enough in medicine: if the patient
dies, the patient has failed; if the patient lives, the physician
has succeeded. *Salus nostra ex Deo; perditio nostra ex nobis.* The
same paradox recurs in all of the professions, in law as in
medicine, in engineering as in public administration; but it
shows itself with special force and incidence in the professions
distinctively called academic, the professions of pure science
and primary scholarship that are practiced in the university. If
a physician errs, his error must before long assail a plain
man's nostril; if an attorney errs, his error must before long
assail a plain man's purse. But if a scholar errs, who shall

name his error? Who, that is, but other scholars, who are at last as unaccountable as he?

The relations of science and government since World War II hang upon this difference. When the Congress of the United States passed the legislation establishing the National Science Foundation, it instituted in effect a fiduciary agency, a formal trust, of which the nation was the intended beneficiary, of which itself acting for the nation was the trustor, but of which scholars—scholars both in and out of government—were inevitably the executants and trustees. Congress and nation can regulate what they are equipped to understand, but in this matter their understanding is strictly limited by the advice of the parties—the community of scholars in and out of government—whose interests are at issue. The scholars have been made judges in their own cause. Effectively, they are beyond the reach of the law; and the government has become, in spite of its theoretical eminence, client in its own domain.

The American disposition is at all times to suppose that where government fails, competition—in this instance, adversary relations among professionals themselves—will supply the unembarrassed corrective. But this belief, whatever may be said of it in other connections, is in this connection a delusion. The professional, though he enters the market, is imperfectly subject to the norm that governs other marketers who have services to sell. If we allow ourselves to speak of doctors and lawyers, and to think of scholars, as engaged in a private practice, it is nevertheless demonstrable that they do not behave as ordinary enterprisers behave. An ordinary enterpriser takes his direction and his rule from the behavior of prices in the market: the objective measure of his service is its value in exchange. A professional, on the contrary, takes his direction and his rule from the collegial fraternity to which he belongs. He may demand in the market whatever he can get, and even sometimes get in the market whatever he demands. But the objective measure of his service is its value before exchange.

Strictly, as a professional assesses his own performance,

the objective value of the service he renders is technical, ep-
istemic, critical—the value, in short, which any other competently informed professional would put upon it, acting in his
place. That representative performance is what he professes to
offer, and what the client who seeks his services expects to
receive—not omniscience, not miracle, not magic, but the service which the professional community, at the present stage of
its technical advance, would authorize. The professional community is presumed to speak through his mouth, to preside in
his judgment, to register itself outwardly in the work of his
hand.

The reliableness of professional opinion varies with the
progress of general knowledge and with the standardization of
formal training in the schools. Nevertheless, at any given stage
of the technical advance of a profession, we cultivate the belief
that the judgment of the compact professional community is
in principle univocal. In a perfectly evolved profession, there
would be no corporals; one member, fully informed, would
judge as every other; and among equally accredited professionals it would be a matter of indifference whose opinion was
invoked. Of course this is not so, and practically we are forbidden to act as if it were. We choose our physicians as we
choose our lawyers, nor does any reflective client suppose that
in choosing one or the other he has secured the risklessness of
omniscience or even the benefits of a constant art. Yet the fact
remains that if, *faute de mieux*, we compete for the services of
professionals, they most assiduously eschew the treasonable
advantages of competing with each other. The capacity to
bring forward the best opinion of the technically informed is
what, after all, both we and they mean by competence in a
profession. Professional competence consists in an ability to
speak, in a given context, with the authority of the professional community. If the professional community's judgment
is not always in fact decided, at least always in principle it is
decidable, according to methods already agreed upon in advance by those who profess to render it. The identifying mark
of an established profession is the assumption, tacitly affirmed

by every professional, that the judgment of his professional community is determinable, and that when determined it affords an objectively authoritative standard of professional performance.

"No scholar or scientist can become an employe in respect of his scholarly or scientific work." [14] The sentence is Thorstein Veblen's. It is the quietest confession of the systematic insularity of the professions that I anywhere know.

Such is the significance of the internal covenant of each of the professional communities, in science as in medicine, in scholarship as in law. Each regards itself as a community set apart; each sets itself apart, by the mutual fealty of its members to each other, from the ordinary competitive conditions of the market economy.

Why do we, who in all other connections rely upon the principle of competition to keep us honest, tolerate this offense against the free market? For the reason that we have no alternative but to tolerate it. The invisible hand practices no medicine, produces no science, demonstrates no theorem, is ignorant of the techniques and processes of the law. The conditions of the market do indeed affect the distribution of professional services; but they do not touch, neither can they influence or certify, the objective value of the services distributed.

That is why, in every civilized society, in the measure that a profession is firmly established, the state will interest itself in certification. In medicine and law the demand is formalized. Before any doctor may practice, before any lawyer may plead, his technical qualifications must be confirmed to the satisfaction of the sovereign. But in this the role of the state is, like that of the market, inevitably passive. The ignorant sovereign does but recognize a right which the learned professions have condescended to institute in its behalf. The right to practice medicine or law is always at last conferred *ex parte* by the learned faculties themselves. Boards of examiners chosen from their numbers grant or withhold certification either with the state's forbearance or under its expressly delegated authority. The lawyer becomes an officer of the court, the physician a licensee; for misfeasance, the one may be disbarred, the other expelled from his privilege. Yet this provision, in which the public interest is vicariously affirmed, though it suffices to license the vicar, is not sufficient to policing his practice. The practice is esoteric; the profession alone is competent to police it; and if the profession will not police it, no one can. The immunity of the professions from effective public control is not merely circumstantial but systematic.

Monopoly, the monopoly of science in the marketplace, is not the problem; the problem is clientism, the clientism of government in its own domain.

For an economic monopoly there is a legislative remedy; for the clientism of the legislature there is none. The legislature affords no remedy for the reason that it is itself among the clients. It delegates responsibilities it cannot own; it certifies commissions it cannot govern. And what is true of the legislative is true also of the executive and judicial branches of government. Armed with all of the external badges of sovereignty, the public power discovers itself to be as abjectly dependent on the autonomous professional communities as ordinary private thee and me.

Talcott Parsons has written: "The professional complex . . . has already become the most important single component in the structure of modern societies. It has displaced first the 'state' . . . and, more recently, the 'capitalistic' organization of the economy. The massive emergence of the professional complex, not the special status of capitalistic or socialistic modes of organization, is the crucial structural development in twentieth-century society." [15]

That is the portentous discovery of our times. The professional is not, except *per accidens*, a capitalist entrepreneur. He is not a worker unionized defensively, for private advantage, in a competitive society. He is not an ordinary government administrator, or a foundation officer, or a bureaucrat. He is none of these. He is, as Emerson saw him, "the delegated intellect," a fiduciary of the larger society, conscious indeed of his professional community as a community that sets itself apart, but conscious also that the community thus set apart has none of the features that belong typically and essentially to what Marx would have described, in his compendious metaphor of social description, as a "class." The class consciousness Marx sought to develop among workers in the labor force is the product of his thinking in the terms of private enterprise. It belongs to an essentially adversarial conception of society of which, to his dying day, he was never able to rid himself. Therefore, to his dying day, he was never able to apprehend, in the rise of the professions, the harbinger of a new order of society.

But this fact escapes us. We are so accustomed to dwelling upon the privacy of the professional that we treat the professions themselves as anarchic enclaves of transmissible privilege in modern society.

The professions have become in fact a part of government, visible branches of the public power. But we persist in committing, with respect to them, the logical fallacy of composition. We suppose that what is true of each of the members of a group must be true also of the group itself; that since the professional has a pocket in his trousers, the profession must be thought to have one too. This delusion, which is reinforced by the legal forms of private property, lies at the root of our failure to understand the relation of science and government in our world. We conceal from ourselves the major constitutional transformation of twentieth-century society.

4. THE PUBLIC COMMISSION OF SCHOLARSHIP
IN GOVERNMENT

The great contemporary problem of science and government is not, as we have supposed, a problem of science; it is a problem of political adjustment, of accommodating autonomous functions, in the ordered peace of one society.

In the medieval world the three great functions of human commonwealth were distributed under the titles *regnum, sac-*

erdotium, and *studium*. Realm, priesthood, university—the first was the domain of the prince; the second of the church; the third of the learned faculties. The division was constitutionally unstable, since in any conflict of authority there was no orderly path of resolution that could be depended on to secure the peace of the commonwealth. Therefore, when, as between pope and emperor, conflicts in fact arose, the coordination fell apart in a competitive struggle for the ascendancy of church or state. Historically, in the secular evolution of modern society, the resolution ran in favor of the realm. A line of demarcation was drawn between jurisdictions. The church was permitted to retain its final voice in matters of faith; the state took to itself the commissions of sovereignty in all matters outward and temporal; and it was assumed, apologetically, that time and eternity would never touch. But the *studium*, the university, remained still to be accommodated, and until the shock of the Reformation it appeared that an accommodation could be had on the same principle. The church condemned the heresy; the state burned the heretic; at such a signal the university would know, by unanimous consent of the faculty, not what to think, but where to be silent. Matters of belief were the unchallenged province of the church, and for so long as the councils of the church remained undivided, priest and scholar found a way to compose their differences peaceably. The state, its prerogatives unaffected, said to its eldest daughter, the parent of the sciences: "So it be that you keep our peace, think as you like, believe as you like, multiply your soliloquies, no man shall diminish your innocent freedom." The difficulty was that, in a church divided, the paths of innocence in matters of belief were no longer clearly defined, and the scholar whose public commission was to seek them out had a Greek Bible on his lectern, a telescope in his hand, and a new method of doubt in his head. He would not keep to his study, much less to his prayerstall. His science was of things temporal; his occupation, with things public. He walked abroad in the realm, in the professions he ministered there, and even when he stayed at home, he made the world

his common. He dared to know it and even, most danger-
ously, to study the prince's place within it. He belonged inex-
terminably to the unhushable profession of Socrates. The only
freedom he claimed or cared for was the freedom that the philosopher Kant viewed as the condition of all legitimate faith or
enlightenment, "the freedom to make public use of one's reason at every point." [16] Public use of reason, not private; its
public use at every point, not only at points politic or decorous
or safe. The public use of reason at every point in human affairs is the modern commission of the university.

   In the circle of the learned professions the community of
scholars—that is, in the enlarged historical sense I have given
to the term, the university both within and beyond the institutional structures that convey it [17]—occupies the central place.
All of the other professional communities without exception
depend upon it and derive their distinctive authority, directly
or indirectly, from the enabling science that it produces. It is
to them what the sun is to its planets, which refract light but
do not generate it.

   The uniqueness of the scientific community is reflected in
the status Congress originally sought to confer upon the National Science Foundation, as it was first conceived. The first
bill passed by Congress (S. 526, 1947) created a new kind of
agency, an agency meant to be viewed as extraordinary, paramount in its own domain, not a department or regulatory office of the executive branch, but a function deliberately set
apart, systematically insulated from the pressure or competition of already existing agencies of government. The bill,
which had passed both houses, was vetoed by President Truman, who asked that its administrative structure be recon-
sidered. [18] The bill placed a matter of paramount public concern under the direction of a part-time board of private
citizens, the scientists outside the mesh of government who
were to be invoked—distinguished, respected, but politically
powerless—to administer it. The President was fully persuaded of the need for an independent foundation; but he was
unwilling to establish any part of government, constitutional

or statutory, that was in principle unwatched and undefended. The question that touched his constitutional duties was not whether the autonomous pursuit of science was a proper part of government but how, without compromise to its autonomy, it might be made responsible to the public interest.

In the National Science Foundation Act of 1950 (Public Law 81-507), an accommodation was reached. The Foundation, as the law now stands, is a statutory agency, not a fourth branch of government. It is neither the only, nor is it even the largest, agency of government concerned with science. By amendment its policymaking functions with respect to the place of science in government have been taken from it. The Foundation has, however, this singularity, which distinguishes it from other agencies, that its relation to the scientific community beyond government is direct, unmediated by special mission. It is "the only Federal agency with an exclusive scientific mandate."[19] It is "independent" of all agencies of government save only the President and the Congress;[20] but its dependence on the university, its systematic assumption that it shall have "the extensive, active cooperation of scientists who are not part of the regular staff of the Foundation", is perfectly unconcealed.

The collaboration of scientists is . . . indispensable in the discharge of the functions of the Foundation. . . . it may well be that we have reached the stage of social development where deliberate collaboration of specialists and concerted development of ideas is possible and necessary. . . . In any event the act requires the Foundation to evaluate scientific progress and to locate fields that need scientific development. . . . Clearly, in embarking upon the problem of evaluation—an undertaking of great delicacy and intricacy in which our society now must pioneer—the collaboration of the scientific community is indispensable.[21]

The university, the community of scholars, has become, by declaration of Congress, "the primary host for fundamental research."[22] in the public commissions of our society.

The university belongs to government in exactly the same way and for exactly the same reasons as the constitutionally recognized primary branches of government belong to it. Each exercises a distinctive and original and complementary function in contemporary polity. Any of the primary branches of government may prohibit the act of the scholar; but no one of them, and not all of them together, may take his place, or assume his function, or preempt his authority, in performing it. And that is all that is intended, operationally, in describing a branch of government as primary, that it is for any rational ordering of human affairs essential, undismissible, and ultimate in its proper authority.

5. THE AUTONOMY OF SCIENCE AND THE RULE OF LAW

Two generations ago it was fashionable to describe the giant industrial corporation—General Motors or Standard Oil of New Jersey or United States Steel—as the representative institution of American society.[23] Everyone consented to the proposition that the market was to our society what the church was to the Age of Faith, or what the belief in the power of natural knowledge was to the eighteenth-century Enlightenment. We were a business civilization, and in a business civilization everyone agrees that what governs the market must be admitted by implication to govern us. Therefore, the representative institution of American society was held to be the industrial corporation, private, anonymous, obscenely powerful, and like any ordinary Yankee sublimely impatient of the restraints of law.

If such a description were to be made today (even among those who heard it yesterday with approval), the person making it would be accused of confusing appearance with reality. The premises of American society may no longer be presumed to lie, either in fact or in theory, in the market. That is perhaps the surest measure of the changes through which, in the present undeclared social revolution of our season, we have passed. All of the great social and political problems of our century carry us beyond the limits of economics. They depend for solution on our ability to make a transition between the private institutions of a pluralist economy and the fiduciary structures, the moral and political arrangements, that coexist with it, and, modify it, and alone can assure its permanence.

Grover Cleveland said of the anarchic concentrations of corporate power in American industrial society: "It is a condition which confronts us, not a theory." Politically, in the modern relations of science and government, the same is true. The principle of social accountability is inoperable in our society, and part of the lawlessness of the modern professions lies in our failure to understand the new place of the university in the national life.

The need for regulating the power of private corporations in a free market remains still with us. But we have in somnolent ignorance allowed ourselves to believe that the problem of collective agency in American life is restricted to the industrial examples we have chosen to analyze. It is not. It recurs with unabated incidence, informal and unnoticed, beyond the purview of the law and the Constitution, in the modern professions. It recurs especially, and nowadays with most fateful confusions, in the community of scholars, in the community without place, which I denominate the university.

The problem of governing the giant and sometimes multinational corporations that populate the modern economy is, if nowhere resolved, at all events everywhere clearly perceived. The problem arises from the inability of government to reach, or, short of reaching, to regulate, the concentrations of private power that it has itself licensed. Astute organizers of industry, long before Cleveland spoke, had apprehended in the legal device of incorporation the clue to a new order of economic activity. Self-perpetuating corporations securely chartered by the public power enabled thousands of scattered shareholders to pool their wealth for private undertakings that would have staggered Egyptian Cheops. Before such colossal enterprises, in former times, even the state would have hesitated. The state is the public corporation, charged with the public interest and responsible for its oversight. But these parlous new actors on the scene—ironmongers, builders of rail-roads, packers of meat—walked private in the shelter of the law, sharing all of the benefits but none of the burdens of public office. Together, the burgeoning corporations commanded the major wealth of the nation; yet, in the silence of the law, no one of them was obliged to concern itself with the social implications of this stupendous piece of intelligence. Each pursued the ordinary advantages, without assuming the ordinary risks, even of a private combination. An ordinary part-nership carries with it the legal implication of *unlimited liability*. Each person entering a partnership stands accountable for the obligations of his legal associates. The advantages of com-bination are therefore always attended, in partnership, by a risk, a risk that can, and at times does, involve one partner in common ruin with another. The device of incorporation fore-stalls this inconvenience by annulling it. A private corporation is grounded on the principle of *limited liability*. The liability of each party to a corporation is measured by his shares of stock; risk is proportioned to ownership; and ownership may be dis-tributed as broadly as the opportunities of private profit can command investment.

The success of this arrangement ran beyond the expecta-tions even of those who profited from it most. Anonymous multitudes, careless of one another, were by law permitted to act together as one person. The ingenuity of the device was incontestable. But its practical effect was to destroy the nexus of traceable responsibility in the social order. In the diffusion of ownership among thousands of transient and absentee shareholders, the police power was unable to reach the actual decision makers into whose hands the powers of massed wealth, affecting the life of the whole society, were concen-trated. The powers of effective decision were delegated to managers, to self-perpetuating boards of directors, who acted in the name of the corporation; responsibility remained with the corporation itself, beneath the obscure shelter of what the French describe, with scandalous lucidity, as the *société ano-*

nyme. The irony of the term is not lost upon us. In the modern corporation the owners come and go; the employee remains and governs.

The late Adolf Berle described this anomaly as "the divorce of ownership from control."[24] As a description of social fact the phrase is faultless. But it fails to convey the constitutional implications Berle and his contemporaries were quick to read into it. A well-ordered society can afford the divorce of ownership from control. Every representative government in the world innocently illustrates that divorce during the term of its elected officers. But no society can afford, even for a term, the divorce of control from responsibility. In American public life a president or a justice is subject to impeachment, a legislator to expulsion. Each is continuously answerable for his acts at the discretion of the parties whom his acts affect. The rule of law assumes this continuity and lapses in the moment that this continuity is broken. The profoundest index of the rule of law in a free society is this unbroken nexus of responsibility for any exercise of power in the public life. And as any break in this nexus is forbidden in the public agencies of government, so also, and even more, it must be forbidden in every private agency. The failure of responsibility to run enforceably in the private sector was the condition of manifest anarchy, of anarchy legitimized, that excited the despair of Cleveland at the end of the last century.[25]

In the anarchic privatism of the modern professions the same hiatus of responsibility under the rule of law prevails. Our legal forms no longer reflect the actualities of our social condition. In the private industrial corporation, especially in those most formidable illustrations of it, the multinationals, the actualities have become manifest. In the community of scholars they remain latent and unexplored, concealed beneath a structure of clientism that we describe without alarm, and without awareness of constitutional anomaly, as the relation of government and science.

The formal divisions of the community of scholars, the divisions we recognize in marking the legal separations between

Princeton and Columbia, Stanford and Chicago, California and Michigan and Cornell—these divisions, predicated on property, private or public, are daily traversed and neglected with impunity by every practicing scholar. The department of knowledge is more consequent than the institution, the discipline more ponderable than the property interest that supports it and claims to own it. For every scholar knows, however society at large may think about the matter, however ambitions for prestige or intellectual association or economic emoluments may lead even scholars to think about it, that the real community, the community that makes a difference in his proper loyalties, lies in no one of these, nor in any parcel of them. Every scholar speaks thoughtful across these boundaries with careless privilege. Ritually, perhaps, in terms of status, these distinctions count for much; intellectually, in terms of the commonwealth of learning, they count for nothing. The economist at Yale speaks more directly to the economist at Wisconsin than either speaks to the historian or man of letters next door; and all speak to each other, in spite of their "two cultures," with clearer voice than any speaks to the state that harbors and accredits their legal separations. Not the legal entity, which is held in fee simple, but the compact community of inquiry, which no one owns, which no one can own for the reason that it belongs permanently in the public domain, is the prime fact of their world.

Formally, this compact community of inquiry has not even the status of a corporation. The law does not recognize it; the written Constitution does not allow it the courtesy of mention. Yet, professionally, it commands the spontaneous allegiance of all scholars, of scholars in government and out of it, of scholars within the nation as of scholars beyond it.

There is, however, a political illusion that accompanies this compact community of scholars. Science, it is said, knows no political frontiers; the laws of physics—indeed the laws of economics, so far as we have such laws—are the same everywhere, in Russia as in China, in America as in Europe and Africa. From this it is assumed that science must lead inevitably to an understanding of human solidarity, that there are, beneath the moral and political divisions that separate us, problems common to all mankind, problems of hunger, problems of population, problems of distribution, problems of preserving the biosphere—problems that, once seen, must cause us to suspend our artificial separations in order to restore, or for once to achieve, a practical conception of the family of man. And it may be so. It may be that a clear apprehension of common problems must produce at last a common conception of one world, in which men shall be at peace, and make plowshares or computers of swords, because they are members of one another.[26] I for one find in this prospect one of the loftiest intimations of the human soul. But I am obliged to state my melancholy belief that the organization of the community of scholars as we know it is not structured to secure this result, to minister to it, or by any necessary mandate to reflect upon it. The claim of the scientific community to an absolute autonomy, its claim to a place beyond politics or government, is now, and has always been, a delusive claim. The claim is delusive because it is, for the purposes of science itself, politically untenable. The pursuit of an autonomous science depends upon the social immunities that permit it, which not it but only a society equipped with its vision can afford. That is why the political responsibility of producing that vision, of educating society to the clear contemplation of it, lies, if not only upon the community of scholars, yet surely upon it, and surely upon it more than upon other breeds or associations of men. The educational function of the university is indivorcible from its research function, not because the two functions are indiscriminable, but because neither without the other can assure its own permanence.

In this matter, it must be confessed, the society thinks more clearly than the scientist. If the Supreme Court strikes down a law of Congress on the ground that Congress is forbidden to enact any law that abridges freedom of speech or of petition or of assembly, it does so from an understanding that the legislative power is necessary even if it is sometimes open to abuse. If Congress impeaches and tries a President for treason, bribery, or other high crimes and misdemeanors in order to determine the propriety of his continuance in office, it does so from an understanding that the executive power is necessary even if it is sometimes misused. The university has not this civilized understanding of the necessity of autonomous commissions other than its own. And until it gains this understanding—that it is free in the web of government, not beyond it—it is not fit to govern in a political order in which all autonomies are complementary, and all therefore are qualified.

Any attempt to qualify the autonomy of the scientific enterprise excites in the minds of scholars the profoundest distrust. In the conduct of his scientific commissions the scholar is the last exponent and most inveterate defender of the operations of the invisible hand in the lives of men and nations. He is content to watch government; he is terrified of being watched by it, terrified of being exposed to the incalculable risks of an external regulation, even at the hands of his own best-informed and most eminent statesmen.

The dangers are real enough. For the power of science is not to be had from politicians. The right estimate of a scientific claim is the proper and perfectly exclusive privilege of the scientific community, and no branch of government may qualify it.[27]

But there is a contrary danger, a danger that in the modern relations of science and government goes unapprehended. For neither, in our times, if we would have science, shall we have it from political absentees, from microbiologists or humanist men of letters or economists, active in the role but passive in the system, who omit to study, and feel no obligation to defend, the fiduciary commission of the university in the total life of our society. Even the best-informed and most eminent statesmen of science will fail if they interest themselves only in the state of science and neglect to cultivate the immunities that permit it to be practiced.

The university is the prime exemplar of the divorce of control from responsibility in modern society. In the relations of science and government this is the *de facto* condition that confronts us, not a theory. No one is so painfully alarmed at the revelation of this condition, or so little disposed by habit and temperament to face it, as the scholar. Yet no one can so little as the scholar afford to neglect it. The scholar is forbidden to neglect it for the reason that no well-ordered society, no society that professes to be under the rule of law, can allow it. The modern scholar is obliged to rethink his place in society, to rethink the system that has for generations allowed him to walk absolved of the direct influences of the market, the church, and the forum. He is obliged to reconceive the political commission of the university, and the meaning of its neutrality, as the public use of reason at every point for society's sake.

We are in danger of repeating Plato's ignorant error, which put the divination of the public good in the hands of the merely expert, as if the rule of law in human affairs were the pure perquisite of intellect, beyond the actions and passions of men, in Plato's heaven. But it cannot be so. The university is a part of government, not a substitute for it. It has not, neither in a democracy can it aspire to have, the authority of a legislature or of an administration or of a judiciary. It legislates no statute, it commands no foot soldier, it decides no question of law under the Constitution. Neither should it. Its basic science is nevertheless, in the informed conduct of our society, the propaedeutic of any of these acts. It has an autonomy equal to that of any branch of government and an authority comlementary to them all.

Henri Bergson, when he was in his eighties, was invited to attend an international congress of scientists. The philosopher of *évolution créatrice* sent his regrets. He was too old, he said, to attend a congress, but not too old, perhaps, to advise one. His advice to his younger contemporaries was so brief that even the young might pause to hear it: "Think as men of action! Act as men of thought!"

That is the role of statesmanship in the modern university, not to secure the fidelity of scientists to the interests of their compact community, but to secure the fidelity of their community to the interests of society at large, whose peace is in their keeping.

NOTES

1. John Maynard Keynes, *The General Theory of Employment, Interest and Money* (New York: Harcourt, Brace, 1936), pp. 383–384.
2. *Gitlow v. New York*, 268 U.S. 652, 673 (1925). Justice Brandeis was party to the dissenting opinion.
3. *The Writings of George Washington, 1745–1799*, edited by John C. Fitzpatrick (Washington, D.C.: United States Government Printing Office, 1940 [1931–1944]), vol. XXXV, pp. 316–317. Cf. Frederick Rudolph, *The American College and University, A History* (New York: Vintage Books, 1962), pp. 42–43.
4. Raymond B. Fosdick, *The Story of the Rockefeller Foundation* (New York: Harper, 1952), p. 141.
5. In 1936 Adolf Berle discovered to America the extremity of the concentration of private wealth wielded for private purposes in the great industrial corporations. Among the great private philanthropies in America the same concentration, wielded for public purposes, repeats itself. "In 1968," says Waldemar A. Nielsen, "some 25,000 foundations of all sizes controlled assets estimated at $20.5 billion. More than half this total was owned by thirty-three general-purpose, grant-making foundations, each with assets of $100 million or more." Even among the giants of the earth who towered above the rest, the distribution was uneven. The Ford Foundation was a lonely Polyphemus. "This prodigal young giant of philanthropy—now in full operation only twenty years—has resources about four times as great as those of Rockefeller and twelve times those of Carnegie. Its assets, which totaled $3.7 billion at the end of 1968, were equal to one-third of the assets of the top thirty-three foundations and one-sixth of those of all 25,000 American foundations." Waldemar A. Nielsen, *The Big Foundations* (New York: Columbia University Press, 1972), pp. 21, 78.
6. U.S. Congress, House, *Hearings before the Committee on Ways and Means on the Subject of Tax Reform*, 91C1 (1969), part IV, p. 1573 (quoted in Nielsen, op. cit., p. 12).
7. Cf. Christian K. Arnold, "Higher Education: Fourth Branch of Government?" 47 *Saturday Review*, (January 18, 1964), pp. 60–61, 75–77.
8. Vannevar Bush, *Science, the Endless Frontier: A Report to the*

President, July 1945 (Washington, D.C.: United States Government Printing Office, 1945), pp. 1–34. The *Report* was received by President Truman; Roosevelt had died in April.

9. Carl Kaysen, *The Higher Learning, the Universities and the Public: The Stafford Little Lectures at Princeton University, 1968* (Princeton, N.J.: Princeton University Press, 1969), pp. 16–19.

10. Don K. Price, *The Scientific Estate* (Oxford: Oxford University Press, 1968 [1965]), p. 37.

11. Carnegie Commission on Higher Education, *A Digest of Reports and Recommendations, December 1968–October 1971* (Berkeley: Carnegie Commission on Higher Education, 1971), p. 9. Cf. Walter P. Metzger, "Academic Freedom in Delocalized Institutions," in *Dimensions of Academic Freedom* (Urbana: University of Illinois Press, 1969), pp. 1–33.

12. Price, op. cit., p. 43.

13. Cf. Christopher Jencks and David Riesman, *The Academic Revolution* (Garden City, N.Y.: Doubleday, 1968 [1969]), p. 517.

14. Thorstein Veblen, *The Higher Learning in America, A Memorandum on the Conduct of Universities by Business Men* (Stanford, Calif.: Academic Reprints, 1954 [1918]), p. 86.

15. Talcott Parsons, "Professions," in *International Encyclopedia of the Social Sciences* (1968), vol. XII, pp. 536, 545.

16. Immanuel Kant, "What Is Enlightenment?" in *Immanuel Kant, Critique of Practical Reason and Other Writings in Moral Philosophy*, translated and edited by Lewis White Beck (Chicago: University of Chicago Press, 1949), p. 287.

17. See chapter I, section 3, above.

18. U.S. Congress, House, Committee on Science and Astronautics, Subcommittee on Science, Research, and Development, *The National Science Foundation: A General Review of Its First 15 Years*, 89th Cong., 2d sess., 1966, House Report No. 1219 (12715-1, 3-1, I), pp. 1–2; Charles V. Kidd, *American Universities and Federal Research* (Cambridge, Mass.: Harvard University Press, 1959), p. 22; Don K. Price, *Government and Science, Their Dynamic Relation in American Democracy* (New York: Oxford University Press, 1962), pp. 48–55; *New York Times*, August 7, 1947, p. 1, col. 5, p. 18, col. 3.

19. U.S. Congress, House, Committee on Science and Astronautics, Subcommittee on Science, Research, and Development, *The National Science Foundation: Its Present and Future*, 89th Cong., 2d sess., 1966, House Report No. 1236 (12715-1, 3-1, I), p. xv.

20. Functionally, the Foundation has identically the kind of independence the Constitution of the State of Michigan confers upon its major state-supported universities (article VIII, sections 4 and 5).

The Constitution provides that the universities shall be directed by their governing boards. The legislature appropriates funds; the boards, which are elected, retain an otherwise exclusive jurisdiction over their internal affairs.

21. Foreword from the Foundation's Annual Report for 1952, quoted in Dorothy Schaffter, *The National Science Foundation* (New York: Praeger, 1969), pp. 34–35.

22. *The National Science Foundation: Its Present and Future*, 89th Cong., 2d sess., 1966, House Report No. 1236, p. 13.

23. Cf. Peter F. Drucker, *Concept of the Corporation* (Boston, Mass.: Beacon Press, 1960 [1946]), pp. 5–11.

24. Adolf A. Berle and Gardiner C. Means, *The Modern Corporation and Private Property* (New York: Commerce Clearing House, 1932).

25. Cf. John F. A. Taylor, "Is the Corporation Above the Law?" 43 *Harvard Business Review* (1965): 119–130.

26. Eugene Rabinowitch, editor of *The Bulletin of the Atomic Scientists*, has written: "Scientists must now assume leadership in establishing the primacy of common interests of mankind over all that divides men into separate camps. Scientists must be pioneers in establishing the one world of man, because theirs is the first common enterprise of mankind, and because this common enterprise has now become the most important content of history." Quoted in *Sponsored University Programs for Research and Education* (Publication No. 12, Office of Research Development and the Graduate School, Michigan State University, East Lansing, 1971), p. 11.

27. Treasury Secretary William E. Simon illustrates the perennial effort to qualify it: "Corporate leaders . . . provide millions of dollars each year to America's educational institutions and foundations. It is fundamental to America's strength to continue that generosity. I would advise, however, that you . . . find out if the subjects of that generosity are really assisting in the fight to maintain our freedoms, or if they're working to erode them. . . . Otherwise the largesse of the free enterprise system will continue to finance its own destruction." *The Chronicle of Higher Education* (March 8, 1976), p. 1, cols. 2–3.

5.

TENURE, COLLECTIVE BARGAINING, AND PUBLIC ACCOUNTABILITY

1. TENURE IN PUBLIC OFFICE

When the President of the United States appoints a justice to the Supreme Court, it must be apparent that in fact, in this exercise of his constitutional authority, he influences the growth of the law. The influence is indirect, since the Constitution that empowers him to administer the law forbids him to make it. The power to influence is, moveover, strictly circumscribed. Under the rule of law the President may appoint judges only "by and with the Advice and Consent of the Senate."[1] Yet, as both he and the senators are aware, even in spite of the most scrupulous efforts to put the interpretation of the law beyond politics, any selection he makes must introduce a new factor into the political equilibrium of the Court. Numerically, the division of the Court may remain constant; qualitatively, it is invariably transformed. Even if we suppose President and Senate to have put aside their partisanships, a new equilibrium is inevitable. The transformation proceeds from the predictable circumstance that the person appointed is himself, in political terms, no cipher. Every new justice brings with him his stamp and temperament, his own judicial proclivities, his own already established conception of the rule of law in our society; and he is in fact chosen for these reasons, not because he is without opinions, not because no stable expectations may be formed of him, but precisely because, in the present composition of the Court, his known propensities are by the President thought necessary, and by the Senate accounted tolerable, if the Court is to preserve an accredited balance in the face of its own and other men's divisions.

Woodrow Wilson used to describe the Supreme Court as a constitutional convention permanently sitting. To appoint a member of the Supreme Court is to name a delegate plenipotentiary to such a convention. At every installation of a new member of the Court, a judge acquires tenure in his office. Tenure is, in the American system, the ax we lay at the foot of the tree. It is a permanent reminder to all the world that the judicial branch of government derives its independent authority, not from the other branches, but from their common root. A new justice is, by the incidents of his genesis, the creature of the President with the consent of the Senate; he is placed in his office with the ordinary expectation that he will preserve in office the same stable opinions he held out of it. But for this tranquil expectancy the Constitution itself makes no stipulation and affords no guarantee. On the contrary, it confers upon the justice a permanently protected privilege which apart from his tenure in office he could not claim. The effect of the formalities that invest him with his authority is precisely to insulate him from the direct influences of those who have been party to his installation or who have opposed it. From the moment at which he is installed, in all matters touching his opinions the Constitution dignifies his independence, not his record; his detachment, not his pedigree. Presidents come and go, Senates are transformed, according to fixed terms of office; they are intended to register the vicissitudes of temporary majorities. But judges—the judges both of the Supreme Court and of the inferior courts—hold their offices, under the Constitution, without limit of time, for life or until voluntary retirement. A judge may be impeached for cause; he may be dismissed from his office for treason or bribery or misfeasance.[2] But his opinions are excluded from the list of admissible causes for impeachment. He is, in the simple letter of the Constitution, irremovable "during good Behavior,"[3] and the quality of his behavior is forbidden to be determined by the opinions he holds, whether or not the opinions he holds consist with the opinions he was expected to hold before he entered into the obligations of his judgeship.

If we ask by what right any mere man should have this unassailable privilege in a democratic society, the answer is clear: By no right whatever. The mere man has no such right; only the occupant of the office has it; and the occupant of the office has it for the good and sufficient reason that the duty of his office requires it. The immunity of a judge in office is the indispensable condition of the rule of law in civil society.

Jurists who have an ear for dangerous paradox take nowadays a certain malicious satisfaction in observing, before persons easily shocked, that the Supreme Court, though it affects only to interpret the Constitution, in fact makes law in the very process of interpreting it. The right to make law, to legislate, is reserved, under the terms of the Constitution, to Congress. Yet, in every case brought before the Supreme Court, in every case of first impression in which, precedent failing, the meaning of the Constitution must be determined in the ultimate tribunal, one of the two litigants is punished *ex post facto*. For until the Court has spoken, the meaning of our fundamental law is simply indeterminate, and the prescribed function of the Court is precisely to determine it, to make known for the case at hand what neither of the litigants could be expected to know independently of the Court's decision. Moreover, in making its decisions, the Court sometimes reverses itself. Does not this accuse its neutral omniscience and betray to us ordinary mortals that it does but legislate, declare *ex parte,* in a forbidden territory, that the rule of law is a fiction and that at last the law is simply what the judges say it is?

There is in this, as in every paradox of the law, an element of truth. Even John Marshall acknowledged as much. The Constitution must, he said, if it is intended to endure for ages, "be adapted to the various crises of human affairs."[4] The demand for adapting the Constitution to the various crises of human affairs Marshall took for granted, as we take it for granted. But "adaptation," as he understood the term, was not to be confused with construction, loose or strict. The strict construction of an indeterminate law must leave it, strictly, indeterminate. To determine it, to adapt it to the various crises of human affairs, is the unfinished work that is left to the Court.

The finishing of the work is not, however, an act of improvisation; it is not an act to be performed in caprice, out of egotism or private sentiment or licentious faction. In a society that professes to be under the rule of law, all judicial interpretation of the law must be strict, all is at last but a reconstruction, the pursuit of an intimation already begun and now again resumed under the same implicit covenant. The interpretation of this covenant in the silence of the written law is the prophetic attempt of men duly appointed to the task, as the fiduciaries of a society, to reappropriate beyond the letter of the law the conception of society that is implicit in its premises. Such is our meaning, when we have a meaning, in marking a distinction between the letter and the spirit of the law. The spirit of the law is its immanent vector, and the preservation of this vector Marshall made the care of judges. "Judicial power," said Marshall, "as contradistinguished from the power of the law, has no existence. Courts are the mere instruments of the law, and can will nothing."[5]

The force of that declaration is heuristic, not dispositive. That is to say, it is the announcement of the obligation we lay upon ourselves in the very act of affirming the rule of law in human affairs. The affirmation of this obligation is necessary in exactly the same sense that the affirmation of the causal principle is necessary for anyone who would inquire into the conditions of our knowledge of nature. Without this principle, which we bring to nature, there could be no knowledge at all. For if I would know the causes of cancer, I cannot afford, in conducting my research, to doubt whether there are in fact causes to be found. This I am obliged to assume, to affirm in anticipation of experience, in order that my research may make any sense at all. The aim of my research is not to confirm the belief that there are conditions upon which, being given, cancer will ensue; the aim is to discover what in particular those conditions are.[6]

Just so, in adapting the Constitution to the various crises of human affairs, the Justice does not permit himself to doubt that there is a critical resolution of his juristic problem. All valid judicial interpretation rests upon this *a priori* claim. When the justices of the Supreme Court argue concerning the meaning of the fundamental law, no single party to the argument holds that an opinion commands consent merely because it has been spoken by a person formally authorized to render an opinion. All alike are thus authorized. That is why argument is necessary. The argument assumes that there is an objectively valid opinion that it is the business of argument to discriminate, and it is this valid opinion that the decision of the Court, in due process, professes to render.

This commonly accredited assumption does not make argument superfluous. It will not of itself dispose of the case at hand. It nevertheless regulates the Court's estimation of any judgment concerning the case. As a justice views his own commission, he performs in the division of the Court a critical act, the burdened act of a fiduciary, obliged to discover, in the silence of the law, its own immanent vector.

To discover that immanent vector at the growing edge of the law is the awesome commission society has delegated to the care of the Supreme Court. If we would be persuaded of this, the times to watch are the times at which the judgment of the Court is divided, the times of imperfect concurrence in which the justices disagree among themselves, in which at least one member of the Court places himself in the role of a dissenting minority. If the Court were free to legislate, any dissent from the majority opinion would count for nothing, as in Congress it counts for nothing and is treated as a mere misadventure of opinion or prediction. But on the contrary, in the rendering of the Court's judgment, the dissenting opinion is included, and the Court is of one mind in requiring it to be heard, as a permanent appendix to its decision. The Court assumes, in one word, that there is a *right* opinion and that no temporary majority, no temporary majority even of its own members, has a prerogative claim upon it. The dissenting opinion is not the aberration of a justice. On the contrary, the preservation of dissent is the Court's public admission of its own liability to error, of the permanent infinality of any of its holdings, since it works always in enthymemes, always in arguments some premises of which are unstated in the written law. Therefore, every argument is precarious; but no properly judicial argument is arbitrary or dismissible.

Let me cite an instance that will raise the question in connection with a manifestly contemporary issue. What has the Constitution to say, with respect to freedom of speech, in the matter of television? Explicitly, it says not a word; implicitly, it must be presumed to declare all that is practically necessary for the right ordering of our affairs. The Court assumes that beneath the letter of the written law there subsists an implicit covenant, the covenant of our society, the permanent articles of agreement that underlie all of our impermanent arguments. That covenant is the law which governs us. It contains all that is "necessary and proper" for the ordered peace of our society. "Let the end be legitimate, let it be within the scope of the Constitution, and all means which are appropriate, which are plainly adapted to that end, which are not prohibited, but consist with the letter and spirit of the Constitution, are constitutional."[7] As the Constitution was originally written, the

Bill of Rights was part only of its immanent vector, which the states demanded to have in writing as a condition of ratification. Let it be asked, Do the first ten amendments extend the meaning of the Constitution? No, they do but articulate it. They supply to it the complement that was already implicit in it, the premises of civility in a free society, which the framers took simply for granted, which the states insisted upon reclaiming from rhetoric, and which the Court still labors faithfully to recover.

The vector of covenant in the instant occasion of history is the despair of all positivists. Marshall cannot be numbered among them. *They* attend only to the letter of the law and to the judicial decisions that appear to extend it; Marshall attends to its immanent vector, to the implied powers not formally deducible from its written part, by which it extends itself. That is why the positivist historians fail always to make any sense of Marshall. They find a statesman, the fiduciary of a covenant, where they thought only to discover a logician or a free legislator. The vector of covenant is nevertheless, for the justice in the Court, his daily fare. It is the whole burden of his argument. And it is sometimes, in the moral confusions of our season, the burden of ours as well. It is the substance which we hear spoken prophetically out of the mouth of a Lincoln or a Jefferson, of a Madison or a Marshall, when they put themselves beyond the divisions that separate us and declare to us the idea of a moral commonwealth, of a society under covenant, into which free men would voluntarily enter and in which they would voluntarily abide. Voices that resonate, imperious comprehending voices that stir in us strange depths, they speak as the old prophets spoke, and as all men are obliged at last to speak, existentially, out of a particular historical situation. They appear to extemporize beyond the letter of the law; but what they speak appeals to our own dumb sense of the moral premises of our society, and what we hear is what already we knew and fully affirmed, but had not the wit to utter, until they declared it.

A judge's tenure in his office has but one justification, to protect society's interest in its covenant. The judge performs a fiduciary function; he must be free to act, without fear or favor, according to the responsibilities his office lays upon him. Therefore, to secure his independence, the Constitution surrounds his office with a shield of permanence it refuses to allow to any other officer. Members of the executive and legislative branches have tenure only for the duration of their terms; they are, so to speak, on permanent probation. That is the fundamental provision of a democratic commonwealth. But for the office of judge the Constitution stipulates no probationary term. Marshall served for thirty-four years and died in his robes at the age of eighty; Holmes served for twenty-nine and retired, still caustic, at the age of ninety-one; William O. Douglas, "the great dissenter," served thirty-six years, the longest term in our history, and having written more than eleven hundred opinions retired physically broken but morally indomitable at seventy-seven.

Even when Roosevelt in 1937 sought to mend the conservative complexion of the Supreme Court's majority by infusing into it new blood, the principle of judicial tenure was never questioned. No justice was to be compelled to withdraw. Roosevelt availed himself of the Constitution's silence on the politically sensitive issue of the size of the Court. The Constitution itself provides only for a Court; the actual size of the body at any time rests upon an act of Congress. Originally, the Supreme Court had six justices; once, during the Civil War, it had ten; today, it has nine, any six of whom may constitute a quorum.[8] Roosevelt, impatient of temporary obstructions, proposed to add an additional justice (to a maximum of six) for each justice then sitting who had passed the age of seventy and, having served ten years, threatened incontinently to live forever.

The proposal was defeated. It fault was not that it offended against the written letter of the law but that it failed to respect its vector. The proposal was, and was meant to be, a challenge to judicial supremacy, a challenge to the supremacy of the judiciary over the other coordinate branches of government. What Roosevelt's outraged contemporaries rejected was the implicit challenge to the rule of law itself. In the ambiguities of the season, as the event proved, this suspicion, if untrue, was nevertheless decisive. But the fact remains that the tenure of judges was at no time, either by Roosevelt or by his most militant supporters, considered a proper subject of challenge. Loyal Americans might legitimately, by the power of appointment and the exercise of a little arithmetic, attempt to overcome the inconvenience of a temporary majority in the Court. But no one presumed to trifle with the tenure of judges. That offense was the surgical remedy the Nazis practiced, in contempt of law, in ruined Germany; its consequences became the disaster of all Europe. During Roosevelt's administration the division of the Supreme Court remedied itself by the ordinary process of our institutions. In American democracy a majority of the Court is an accident of politics; the tenure of justices is a necessity of the office delegated to their care.

2. THE TENURE OF THE SCHOLAR

I have been at pains to describe the fiduciary function of justices of the Supreme Court for one reason only, that here, in the judicial system, we encounter the principle of tenure in public office in its purest, most articulate, and most universally accredited form. The tenure of judges affords a paradigm for understanding the institution of tenure in the university.

An accredited paradigm is nowadays, in the university, most urgently needed. The institution of tenure in the university comes under an open and sustained public criticism that threatens to cancel it in principle. By what right, it is asked, shall any class of men, performing acts of public consequence, be permanently released from public probation? The tenure of university professors excites in many minds the bitterest and most determined opposition. They see in it an unwarranted and unwarrantable social distinction, an ascriptive privilege smelling of aristocracy, inessential to the interests of scholarship and sometimes destructive of its larger purposes. The challenge a democratic society raises, and must indispensably raise, against every unwarranted privilege, deserves an absolute respect; and no serious scholar, no scholar who understands the public obligations of his office, will fail to afford it. Unless the tenure of the scholar is warrantable on considerations of the public interest, there is no defense of it, and can be none. But we have grown accustomed to meeting the challenge to tenure with self-serving arguments that confuse, and invite the public to confuse, tenure with job security. We draw our defense neither from the language of the law nor from the traditions of the academy; we draw it from the language of collective bargaining and the industrial labor contract. That is why the original paradigm of tenure in public office needs to be invoked. A justice of the Supreme Court has in fact a security in his job. But it is a mistake to suppose that the tenure of judges is established in order to produce that contingent personal benefit. The private benefit that is incidental to tenure must be distinguished from the public benefit that alone can justify it. The motive that animates society in establishing the tenure of judges is not that the judge may be permanently employed but that the society which employs him may be disinterestedly served.

Academic tenure rests upon the same foundation. It is not the labor, it is the labor in the public service, that establishes the scholar's moral claim. Fritz Machlup says, "Really, the only justification for the system of academic tenure lies in the social products of academic freedom."[9] The scholar, like the judge, performs the duties of a fiduciary in the public service. He is granted tenure, not because society interests itself in the permanence of his job, but because society needs indispensably to be assured, in all matters touching the truth of his opinions, of the independence of his judgment. Clark Byse and Louis Joughin have written:

The ultimate beneficiaries of academic freedom are not those who exercise it but all the people. . . . Academic freedom and tenure do not exist because of a peculiar solicitude for the human beings who staff our academic institutions. They exist, instead, in order that so-

ciety may have the benefit of honest judgment and independent criticism which otherwise might be withheld because of fear of offending a dominant social group or transient social attitude.[10]

The nearest approximation to a definition of the meaning
of tenure in American institutions of higher learning is a statement of principles set forth in 1940 by the American Association of University Professors (AAUP) and the Association of
American Colleges.[11] The AAUP's original 1915 Declaration of
Principles remains the Association's primary document, the
brilliantly argued exposition of all of its larger purposes;[12] the
1940 Statement of Principles on Academic Freedom and Tenure is
but a working extension of it, an effort to define for general
consent the meaning of acceptable practice under its terms.
The 1940 Statement has become, in all practical connections
concerning tenure, the standard interpretation of the norms of
the profession. Eighty-one learned societies, among them
some of the most distinguished congregations of intellect in
American life, have since 1940, by formal endorsement, added
to the Statement the weight of their authority.[13] Today, it is
without question the single most important declaration on the
subject of tenure in American education.

"Institutions of higher education," says the 1940 Statement, "are conducted for the common good." Society, not the
scholar or the community of scholars—"not . . . the individual teacher or the institution as a whole"—is the beneficiary of
the university's public commission. The university claims no
privilege that cannot be validated on grounds of its service in
the public cause. It asks but one concession as the condition
of its service, the consent of society to the Jeffersonian proposition that "the common good depends upon the free search
for truth and its free exposition."[14]

The framers of the Statement do not profess to offer a justification of this pronouncement. On the contrary, they apprehend in it, as Jefferson apprehended in it, a principle, a pos-
tulate, the foundation of argument, from which all
justifications must proceed. The dependence of the common
good on the free search for truth and its free exposition is the

radical affirmation of an open society. It is the profoundest paradox of such a society that it will risk freedom in order to have it. An open society will tolerate any risk in matters of belief in order to secure understanding in matters of practice. Every society professes to affirm the common good; an open society dares to go critically in search of it.

The right of free inquiry that is the breath in the nostrils of all science is but a specialized extension of the general rights and immunities conferred by the First Amendment of the Constitution of the United States, as the Supreme Court now interprets it.[15] Membership in a free society is not a hammock; it is not a sinecure. It carries with it the ineffaceable obligation, which lies upon all citizens, to make of the conditions of their moral community their common care. The Constitution is erected "in order to form a more perfect union, establish justice, insure domestic tranquillity, provide for the common defense, promote the general welfare, and secure the blessings of liberty to ourselves and our posterity."[16] Therefore, Congress is forbidden to make any law abridging the freedom of speech, or of the press, or the right of the people peaceably to assemble. For if the common good depends upon the free search for truth and its free exposition, then whatever can be shown to be an indispensable condition of the free search for truth and its free exposition must be by right afforded.

Such is the general force of the First Amendment. It bears this special consequence, that if in the division of our labors the search for truth must be in some of its parts delegated (as in the courts it is expressly delegated in matters touching the law itself), then upon those to whom the duty of search is transmitted, the same enabling freedom must be by right conferred.

The scholar's right of tenure is not original but derivative; it proceeds from the obligation of those whom we have commissioned to perform the tasks of inquiry; they must be free to do what by delegation they are required to do. In his private capacity, a scholar may think or speak without benefit of

tenure. Tenure does but confirm the public interest in his private office. Formally, it is society's commissioning of the delegated intellect, society's formal declaration that it conceives
the public interest to lie in the uninterrupted freedom of the
scholar's performance and will, if his freedom is threatened,
act to protect it.

That is the sum of the *Statement*'s argument. The institution of tenure is the first prerequisite of the freedom of scholarship conceived as a public office. If we in fact affirm the vir-
tues of an open society; if we affirm our society's interest in
securing for itself, in matters of belief, the benefits of an unrestricted criticism; if in a word we subscribe to Kant's vision
of enlightenment, "the freedom to make public use of one's
reason at every point," then by that affirmation we at the same
time undertake, necessarily, the duty of sheltering the agents
who are by delegation commissioned to perform the tasks of
inquiry. Our motive in establishing the immunity of scholars
is identical with our motive in establishing the immunity of
judges, namely, in order to have, in the public interest, the
benefits of an unfettered research. Nothing—nothing in
heaven or earth—obliges us to affirm the openness of society.
Either we oblige ourselves, or we walk unobliged, slaves by
omission. But if we oblige ourselves, tenure is that obligation.

Strictly, the public commission of scholarship is vested in
the university, that is, in the chartered community of scholars,
into which the individual scholar is admitted and in which by
virtue of tenure (probational or permanent) he acquires a formal status. The tenured scholar performs his public duties by
a secondary act of delegation; the primary delegation, in
which society can properly be asked to interest itself, runs to
the university, to the community of inquiry, which society
charters and agrees to tolerate. Society commissions the university; the university, by the device of tenure, confers membership in itself.

Fustel de Coulanges used to say to his hearers: "Do not
applaud me: it is not I that addresses you, but history that

speaks through my mouth." The grandiloquence of that phrasing may perhaps offend against the demands of ordinary modesty. The audacity of the speaker needs, perhaps, forgiveness. Nevertheless, that sentence bears the thrust, if not the accomplishment, of all scholarship whatever. Fustel claims for his voice a prophetic authority. He claims to be the disinterested and neutral spokesman of an erudition quietly funded out of the exchanges of scholars everywhere. What the learned Fustel speaks, if history speaks through his mouth, is, beyond all egotism, what equally would be spoken by any other scholar equally informed. History is what the historians say it is? It is, as Voltaire described it, but "a fable agreed upon"? No, the fable agreed upon is, at any stage of our progress, the topic of argument, not its verdict. At any stage of historical understanding all that we have is the vector of argument in the tribunal of the competently informed. It is possible to think beyond that tribunal, and I suppose the world-shattering reflections of any age are those in which lone scholars have sublimely dissented from the received opinions, the fables agreed upon, of their scholarly contemporaries. But that is only to say that the voice of the tribunal is in any season the voice of a temporary and precarious majority, and in all seasons liable to error, which the tribunal is, for the time being, unwilling or unable to mend. The tribunal of the competently informed is nevertheless, in the imperfection of our condition, the best that we are capable of. Every dissenting opinion is at last addressed to it and is obliged to establish itself in the face of its contrary holdings. It is capable of monstrous error; yet it harbors also the critical resources by which error is mended. For its genius is that it institutionalizes the argument, never the fable. We oblige ourselves to wait upon the results of an open process that, given time and tolerance, will correct itself. To preserve and defend that process—the process, not the fable agreed upon—we commission the tribunal. Tenure is the formal delegation of its offices.

But that, if it is understood by scholars, is not the public understanding, and it must be admitted that the effort, of late years, to establish the collective bargaining powers of the faculty has confused both the public and the profession itself.

Tenure [says the *Statement*] is a means to certain ends; specifically: (1) Freedom of teaching and research and of extramural activities and (2) a sufficient degree of economic security to make the profession attractive to men and women of ability. Freedom and economic security, hence, tenure, are indispensable to the success of an institution in fulfilling its obligations to its students and to society.[17]

The two "ends"—freedom of inquiry and the economic security of the inquirer—command a very unequal authority in the public notice. Economic security is a contingent benefit of tenure that runs to the private advantage of the scholar. Academic freedom is the essential benefit that runs to the public advantage of society. Society concerns itself only with the latter. It concerns itself, as it concerns itself in the appointment of judges, with the fiduciary role of the professional which is public, not with the personal role of the marketer which is private. No one, at least no one competently informed concerning the premises of a democratic society, will question the public interest in the free search for truth and its free exposition. But there are now, and have always been, many who question the obligation of society to guarantee the permanent economic security of the member of a profession. Lawyers and physicians, who work privately, make no such claim; nor could such a claim, if it were made, be properly allowed. The question is not whether the labors of the legal and medical professions conduce in fact to the public welfare. Undeniably they do. Yet, in the measure that lawyers and physicians work privately, they are obliged to endure the risks of privacy. No professional, in his strictly private capacity, can escape those risks; nor can government, the government either of a profession or of society at large, absolve him of them. His economic security is his own affair. Why should it be otherwise with the community of scholars? For one reason only, that they are engaged in a public work—in the public affair, the *res publica*, as we used to say. Scholars, like judges, are fiduciaries burdened with the duties of a public office and must be immunized from interference or reprisal in the performance of it, lest the office itself be canceled.

The ideal of service in the public interest is by no means restricted to the scholar's profession; it is the foundation of any moral claim to autonomy on the part of any profession whatever.[18] But the economic security of the scholar (such as it is) is not a matter of claims; it is a matter of social necessity, which an open society must afford, whether or not scholars bethink themselves to claim it. Scholars, like judges, are granted economic security, not because they ask it, or have the power of exacting it, but because society requires it, in the interest of securing to itself the benefits that flow from the free search for truth and its free exposition.

3. THE PRACTICE OF IMMUNITY

If by the tenure of university professors one intends a system of tenure commonly agreed upon and uniformly applied in all American institutions of higher education, then, it must be admitted, there is no such system.[19]

The variations of practice in both public and private institutions—we have some 2,543 of them in the national scene—are very broad. Nowhere is the pluralism of American institutions so manifestly declared. Some institutions refuse to admit tenure in any form. A professor in a private college may wear the dignity of his academic title at the pleasure of a lay board that contracts for his services as it contracts for the services of an employee who has no such title. There are, however, institutions of unblemished privacy in which the articles of tenure are so firmly secured by ancient unwritten precedents that it would be unthinkable to override them, though a million-dollar bequest depended on it. At others, the board lays explicit limits on its own chartered powers of arbitrary dismissal; the rules of tenure take the form of a written policy, adopted by the governing board and included by reference in its contracts. State-financed institutions grant tenure by an exercise of powers vested in them by law. The tenure policy of a state institution has the force and effect of statutory law enacted by the legislature or of administrative rules adopted by a governing board that draws its authority directly from the state constitution.

Yet, in spite of all complications and exceptions, the fact remains that 94 percent of all faculty members in American universities and colleges work at institutions that confer tenure in some form. What are the conditions that are essential to it? What, in the modern community of scholars, is the implicit norm, the norm implicitly affirmed, wherever the principle of tenure prevails?

Academic tenure is the right conferred by a university upon a faculty member—either immediately or after a limited period of probationary service—to continue in membership in the faculty of the university until retirement or until, under the rules of academic due process, adequate cause has been shown for his suspension or dismissal.[20]

A federal judge acquires tenure in his office immediately upon his installation; no date is fixed for his retirement, and he may, if he chooses, continue in office until he dies. A young scholar, at the threshold of his career, has no such immediate guarantee. He gains his initial admission into the faculty of a university only for a fixed term. The term varies with institutions; but it is understood that the right of permanent tenure is reserved, that the instant appointment is probationary, and that continuance in temporary status or advancement to permanent status is the subject of a separate decision, which has still to be taken.

Nevertheless, though the appointment is limited in time, the new member is for the period of his probation party to the privileges, as he is party to the obligations, of the academic community. His permanence in the ranks of the faculty remains still to be decided; but his essential freedom—the freedom of research and exposition—is already confirmed. Any assault upon his privilege under the covenant of the university will be deemed an assault upon the freedom of the university itself. Least among his peers, he stands nevertheless among them; and he shares with them, for the fixed period of his appointment, an equal immunity. For that period (though formally only for that period) he is, like the most exalted of his tenured colleagues, irremovable during good behavior. Let him perform the duties reasonably assigned to him, his right of dissent against any received opinion will be sustained, even though the dissent may run against those who are taxed to sustain it. The university may regret the extravagance of his opinions; it may or may not choose to renew his office; but it may not deny him the freedom that is the perquisite of his office, so long as he holds it. The defense of that perquisite is the university's permanent commission. A university that denies unconditional freedom of opinion at the threshold of inquiry has already denied it at every later stage.

The *1940 Statement* forbids that the probation should be without limit of time. "At the expiration of a probationary period, teachers or investigators should have permanent or continuous tenure, and their service should be terminated only for adequate cause, except in the case of retirement for age, or under extraordinary circumstances because of financial exigencies."[21] The *Statement* omits to stipulate a minimum for the period of probation;[22] it recommends a maximum period of seven years: "The probationary period shall not exceed seven years, including within this period full-time service in all institutions of higher education."[23]

This provision is one of the most remarkable, as it is one of the least understood, articles of the theory of tenure. From it has emerged the administrative policy, that a scholar must at the expiration of his probationary period be advanced to permanent status or dismissed: he must, as the saying goes, move "up or out." Probationers universally regard this provision with fear and trembling. We measure (they say) tragedy by water clocks. Inevitably the length of the season of probation is arbitrary; always it is mechanical; sometimes it is punitive, the blind sacrifice of Iphigenia to the silly movement of a fleet. Yet still, by everyone's admission, a limit is necessary.

If the university is willing to wait forever, the scholar cannot, and the stipulation of a reasonable maximum serves in fact the public interest. At a time agreed upon, the rule exacts a decision. It requires an institution to declare, and forbids it to conceal, what the scholar needs indispensably to know, its opinion of his fitness, in the long run, to be full party to its public commission. A scholar's probation is not an unlimited indenture; it is not a tacit consent to servitude. The institution's interest is defended, after all, by the minimum period of probation, a period that it, itself, sets. The maximum period—the "up-or-out" provision—forbids only that any member of the academic profession should find himself wearing, at the ragged end of his career, the afflicting title of Teaching Fellow Emeritus.

The provision that the probationary period must include full-time service in all institutions of higher education is another matter. It is in fact the manifesto of a profession, the frank declaration on the part of scholars that they are, in spite of the separation of their parishes, of one house and covenant. The community of scholars transcends the parochial limits of any local center of scholarship—of Swarthmore or Princeton, of Oberlin or Chicago, of Pomona or Berkeley. The local centers are many; the community is one, one society of professionals bound together under a single covenant of inquiry, which remains constant beneath their comings and goings. Therefore, since the community is served wherever the covenant runs, service in one center must count as service in another. This principle is essential to the conception of tenure in the community of scholars. Practically, however, in the American system of higher education, the power of conferring tenure lies decisively with the local centers. The community of scholars has no purse, and it is perhaps just as well that it has none. But the practical consequence of its having none is that the conditions of a scholar's employment are set, not by the community of scholars, but by the legal enclaves, the local centers of scholarship, into which they congregate. These centers—Pomona, Oberlin, and Swarthmore; Princeton, Chicago, and Berkeley—decide the conditions of tenancy in themselves. The result is a collision of principles, a collision of the principle of solidarity, which is essential to the profession, with the principle of local autonomy, upon which the legal divisions of our institutions are founded. In our actual practice, the principle of autonomy takes precedence. Credit for prior service in the profession is transferable only by consent of the local community, by consent of the institution into which the scholar seeking employment would gain admission. More than half of our institutions allow no credit for prior service. Among the two-year colleges and public four-year colleges, for every three that allow credit there are seven that disallow it; among the institutions in which the principle of professional solidarity is most liberally conceded—the universities and the four-year private colleges—only six out of ten allow it.[24] The system of collegiality and the system of employment are, in the fabric of American higher education, imperfectly reconciled, and nowhere is the collision of the two systems so patently visible as in the terms of probation.

The *1940 Statement* contains no provision for a required minimum period of probation. As events have demonstrated, the omission is critical, and its consequences now threaten the institution of tenure itself. In the season of unabated expansion that followed World War II, institutions of higher education put aside their old and stable patterns of employment in order to accommodate the unprecedented demands that were made upon them. Enrollments were exorbitant; qualified personnel were in painfully short supply; and the local centers of scholarship, which competed for their services, did not hesitate to exchange the permanent entitlements of tenure for a temporary release from emergency. No one imagined that the mandate of a great society to educate itself would ever cease. And indeed it has not. But the failure to stipulate a reasonable minimum period of probation has resulted, in the absence of any countervailing administrative policy, in a systematic concentration of personnel in the upper, formerly the least populous, ranks. The rank of instructor has virtually disappeared

from use; the rank of assistant professor, once exclusively probational, may now on occasion command all of the perpetui-
ties of tenure without benefit of a doctor's hood. The upper
ranks have not escaped. Young dauphins, impeccably qualified, who formerly waited for succession in the antechambers,
now populate the throne rooms of the university. They will
continue in occupation of their tenured offices for a longer period than formerly. About 50 percent of all faculty have permanent tenure. Tenure is, however, in the practice even of
some major institutions, awarded to from 60 to 80 percent, or
more, of those eligible to receive it. Since the higher salaries
are attached to the tenured ranks, the fixed cost of maintaining
the same establishment has risen. This consequence, tolerable
so long as the size of faculties was expanding, is no longer
tolerable when the size of faculties contracts or remains constant. Under a fixed income, the only contraction of program
that is possible must fall upon the untenured who, having no
place to go in the institution, must therefore go out of it. The
scythe of time that once abbreviated a hateful subordination
now artificially maintains it; and the young, who once lived
only in the shadow of their elders, live now in the shadow of
each other.

But suppose these difficulties in the practice of tenure to
be got over, suppose permanent tenure to be at last conferred,
What does permanence imply?

A person in permanent or continuous tenure is not immune to dismissal. Neither, if the university is held accountable to the public interest, should he be. A tenured member
of the faculty may be dismissed "for cause." But he may not
be dismissed except for cause; the cause must be "adequate";
and the burden of establishing adequate cause lies on the institution that employs him. For so long as a member of the
faculty holds his position in probationary appointment, his
continuance beyond the fixed term of his office depends
(within the limits of due process) on the willingness of the
governing board to renew his appointment: the burden of establishing a right to continue in the employment of the insti-

tution lies on him.[25] But in the moment that a faculty member acquires tenure, the burden shifts. The normal presumption is that a tenured faculty member will be continued; and it now lies on the institution to establish that there are compelling reasons, affecting the defense of academic freedom itself, for displacing him and disturbing the normal expectations of the academic community.

That there are in fact such reasons, "legitimate grounds for dismissal" that may, on proper showing, warrant the removal of a tenured member of the faculty, has never been doubted. It has never been doubted even by those who insist most strenuously on job security. Every significant claim to tenure is based upon a presumption of good behavior; every legitimate defense of such a claim is based upon an understanding that the academic community is willing to order its own house, to police the competency of its practitioners and their faithfulness in the discharge of their duties, for society's sake. The obligation to police itself in exchange for its privilege is the first condition of a free community of scholars, of the "delegated intellect," in human affairs. Free scholarship is indivorcible from social responsibility.

The original covenant of the American Association of University Professors, the *Declaration of Principles of 1915,* announces the need for an explicit enumeration of causes for dismissal. The enumeration was left, however, to individual institutions.[26] As the framers of the *Declaration* viewed the priorities of the profession, the first need was not to codify causes of dismissal but to obtain the consent of all parties to the essentials of due process, to rules commonly admitted and commonly adhered to, wherever cause was to be shown. No tenured professor, whatever the cause, was henceforth to be dismissed without a formal hearing before his academic peers. Let this be granted, the enumeration of causes could be studied in the fullness of time. The demand for a definition of "adequate cause"—for a definition commonly accepted by the profession and by the employing institutions—has never in fact been met. Harvard University lists but two grounds for dismissal, "grave misconduct or neglect of duty"; Stanford lists "substantial and manifest incompetence", "serious and protracted disability, or protracted absence without leave", and "extraordinary financial emergency."[27] There are longer lists than these; but these will do, and I know no scholar who would not, under the firm guarantees of academic due process, accept them. The composition of the lists is less important than the fact that such lists, capable of commanding the general consent of scholars everywhere, can be brought forward. But the paramount interest of all such lists lies elsewhere. It lies, unspoken but obligatory, in the vector of the covenant of a free scholarship. Universally, in passing judgment on their peers, scholars will exclude freedom of opinion from any list of possible grounds for dismissal. That is the danger, it is also the glory, of the community of scholars in a democratic society, that they refuse to allow, as a condition of good behavior, any limit on the range of opinions they are prepared to tolerate in the free search for truth and its free exposition. A scholar's opinions are not an admissible cause for challenging his membership in the academic community.

Nothing in the conception of tenure puts professors beyond the reach of the law or beyond the ordinary boundaries of public accountability. They labor as fiduciaries in the public interest and are as amenable to judgment for misconduct or neglect of duty as any other person who is entrusted with the exercise of a public office. All that the institution of tenure requires is that the judgment be made on proper grounds, on grounds that are consistent with the free search for truth and its free exposition, by persons competent to judge of the technical conditions of performance in that enterprise. Let a professor act within the limits implied by that purpose, let him perform the obligations that are essential to the free winnowing of opinion, tenure will shield him. It will shield him though he offend against the views most sacredly held in his society. But let him exceed or leave undone the duties of his office, he betrays his privilege and relinquishes the right of immunity that belonged to him as member of the community of free scholars.

4. COLLECTIVE BARGAINING AND THE COLLEGIALITY OF SCHOLARS

In 1971, the original sponsors of the *1940 Statement*—the Association of American Colleges and the American Association of University Professors—joined in instituting a special commission to examine the actual operation of tenure in the American scene. The Commission on Academic Tenure in Higher Education was chaired by William R. Keast of the University of Texas and is commonly identified by his name as the Keast Commission. Sustained by a grant from the Ford Foundation, the commission was instructed to design and execute its own independent study. To assure its independence, it was charged to report directly to the academic community and to the general public without reference to its sponsors.

The *Report of the Keast Commission* is the most comprehensive study of the *de facto* institution of tenure in American society. It finds the institution in grave jeopardy, beset by social forces both within and beyond the university, that threaten to extinguish it. Unremedied, its errors will cause it to wither; concealed, its shortcomings will cause it to be disowned. Yet, notwithstanding all of its manifest defects, the commission regards this beleaguered institution as the most reliable instrument for the defense of academic freedom in our society. The preservation of the institution of tenure in American society will, however, depend upon the readiness of the community of scholars to work at its reformation. Reformation there must be, and the need for it is urgent. An uncritical retention of the system in its present pattern will destroy the system; and if amendment comes not from within the scholarly community, it will come most certainly from without, from social and political and economic forces that are ignorant or careless of the stakes at wager in the public life.

Ironically, in our season, the major threat to tenure comes from within the university itself. It comes from the rank and file of scholars, from men and women within the walls who seek to reform, not tenure, but the terms and conditions of their employment. Typically, they treat the community of scholars as an extension of the labor market. They confuse tenure with job security, the trusteeship of a society with an occupational guarantee. The confusion of tenure with job security has had the effect of dividing the academy against itself, transforming complementarities of function into conflicts of interest. In the ancient tradition of the community of scholars, if, for instance, two members of the law faculty disagree, or the faculty of law opposes itself to the faculty of arts, or the gathered faculties take a stand against the administration, it is tacitly understood by all individuals who are party to the division that they stand opposed as colleagues, not as enemies or strangers. Beneath their rivalry is their common purpose; beneath every statutory argument, a constitutional agreement. Collegiality is the norm; and every conflict is presumed to be a loyal aberration from it, for which there must be a remedy in due process. This presumption may prove to be in some connections false. All of the great historical contests over academic freedom and tenure have in fact arisen from divisions in which this presumption has been held in doubt; every restoration of peace has flowed in fact from its reaffirmation. In the community of scholars collegiality is everywhere assumed until its absence has been shown. That is why the adversary relations that are typical of the labor market—the conflicts of management and labor, of supervisor and wage earner, of employer and employee—never quite fit the traditions of the academy. The substitution of adversarial for collegial relationships in the modern academy represents in fact, in the language of the Keast Commission, a "breakdown" in the system.[28] The manifest symptom of this substitution is the institution of collective bargaining.

I should perhaps say at once that there is no necessary incompatibility between the institution of tenure and the in-

TENURE AND COLLECTIVE BARGAINING 157

stitution of collective bargaining. Medieval universities set lucid precedents. They bargained aggressively to win, they
struck unashamedly to maintain, in sight of king and com-
mune, the recognition of their privileges. The *magna carta* of
the University of Paris—Pope Gregory IX's bull *Parens scientia-
rum* ("Mother of sciences," 1231)—contains phrasings reminis-
cent of the tavern brawl of which it was the late beneficial
product. It ended the Great Dispersion of the Paris masters, a
strike lasting two years, in which offended clerks demonstrated, with political implications worth pondering, the
power of scholars to withhold their services pending the establishment of fair employment practices. The University of
Padua owes its upstart foundation to a student boycott of Bologna, begun in protest, confirmed in secession, made permanent by emigration (1222). Venerable Cambridge, which we
put beyond the vicissitudes of violence, was born of an Oxford
strike, the *suspendium clericorum* of 1209, in which the faculty
of Oxford carried its lectures elsewhere, set up house in
marshlands, extorted a new contract from the astonished Oxford burgesses, and turned its learned attentions to some of its
own members, whom it penalized for scabbing. Tenure and
collective bargaining are not mutually repugnant. Historically,
in fact, the one has arisen from the other. "The masters,"
wrote Hastings Rashdall, "lived on their own misfortunes."

But these events belonged to our salad days, when we
were green in judgment. Tenure and collective bargaining, in
spite of the incidents of their evolution, rest on different assumptions concerning the place of the scholar in society; and
it is indispensably necessary, at the present juncture of our
history, that they be seen as separate. Tenure rests on the assumption that scholarship is a public commission which society shelters in the public interest; collective bargaining on the
assumption that scholarship is a private vocation which scholars shelter in their own interest. Both assumptions are innocent; both may be true. The lay public, which supports the
university, contemplates the benefits to itself of the free search
for truth and its free exposition; the scholar, who occupies the

university and performs its public offices, contemplates the benefits to himself of job security.

The American scholar performs a public function; he makes a private living at it. Outwardly, the two activities coincide, and in this particular the scholar's role is like that of any other public employee—fireman or policeman or sanitation worker—who makes his living in the public service. But this coincidence of public commission and private livelihood, which is sufficiently certified in the terms and conditions of the policeman's or the fireman's or the sanitation worker's employment, has, in the person of the scholar, no formal guarantee. Public employees—policemen, firemen, sanitation workers—are allied to each other by virtue of their employment; professors, by virtue of their calling. The system of collegiality that unites the community of scholars is distinct from the system of employment that distributes their services. The scholar who sees himself only as an employee is therefore permanently exposed to the error of believing that if the system of employment is properly attended to, the system of collegiality will automatically develop out of it. The simple fact is that it will not. Tenure is our systematic effort to institute that relationship.

Samuel Gompers, asked to formulate the aims of organized labor, restricted himself to one word: "More." Sentimental moralists have always despaired of that phrasing; cynical economists have always delighted in it. But Gompers himself was neither sentimentalist nor cynic. He performed for his contemporaries what was in fact, in the multitudinous contexts of the American labor market, a brilliant act of abstraction. He educated workers to see, beyond all their differences from each other, beyond the material circumstance that one stokes the furnace and another works the forge, the identity of their purposes in a competitive economy—namely, higher wages, shorter hours, and job security. No bookish scholar shall, by an elegance of phrase, diminish the gravity of that perception. If industry is structured on adversarial relations; if society reduces the terms of the human encounter to the faceless estrangements of collectivities; if our social bond with each other is but the demoralized product of the juxtaposition of egos in one neighborhood, then everything, for each of us, must at last depend on the right calculation of private advantage. A laborer must be taught to understand that his proper opponent in the market is not the laborer who works beside him, who like himself has only his labor to sell. The laborer beside him is, in any strict calculation of his private interest, his natural ally. All that they have in common may be their opposition to management; yet, having only this, they may be led to see that together they wield a power that neither wields separately. The individual laborer, if he contracts directly with management for the sale of his labor, bargains from an unequal position. He is not free not to sell, since any part of his labor that is offered but unsold is irrevocably wasted, wasted as irrevocably as the power of a stream that flows unused to the sea. Therefore, individually, the laborer is powerless, since management governs, and is free unilaterally to withhold, employment. But if laborers can be brought to bargain as one body, negotiating a single contract for the exchange of their collected labors, management will be found from that moment to depend as abjectly on them as they on it. Management may dispense with the services of the individual laborer; it cannot dispense with the services of another to labor in his place; and the capacity to command the refusal of any other to labor in his place is the demonstrable advantage—what John R. Commons used to describe as the "opportunity value"—that an organized labor force is equipped to realize. What is the opportunity value that Gompers saw in the device of collective bargaining? A difference in the terms and conditions of labor and an increased share in its social product.[29] Collective bargaining is the individual's private path to higher wages, shorter hours, and job security.

And is not this opportunity value available to scholars as to other varieties of men? It is. It is as available to them as to any other class of laborers, and some indeed have seized upon it as an incentive that is not only fitting and decent but inevi-

table for the development of the university under modern conditions. The American economy trembles always on the razor's
edge of substituting condemnation for consent, lonely privacy
for public morality, status for contract. If society at large will
not afford, or by the terms of the market forbids, participation
in a common life, then men will frame limited mutualities
within it, putting their loyalties where their lives are led and
their freedom where their fellowships are found. Why should
not scholars attempt to secure to themselves the advantages
and emoluments that accrue to lawyers and medical practitioners, and for that matter to steamfitters and teamsters and gar-
ment workers, by the simple expedient of not competing with
each other in the sale of their services?

The question is by no means frivolous, and it is a mistake
to suppose, in a society that has allowed itself to think of its
total life in terms of adversarial relations, that the piety of disinterested scholarship will cause every other piety, including
the redemptive piety of economic security, to be set aside. The
other pieties will not be set aside; neither, in a society that
professes to dignify the individual, can they be. The demand
to respect the public interest in the private calling is nothing
peculiar to scholarship; it belongs to American institutions
generally, even to the institution of the free market, wherever
that institution is obedient to the larger covenant of our society. What the American political covenant dignifies is the individual, not the collectivity. But in this exercise of reverence
for the individual we are guilty of a perennial confusion. We
confound individuality with privatism, dignity with separateness, freedom with isolation. The proper subject of dignity in
a democracy is the individual *in* the common life, not beyond
it, not apart from it, not in spite of it. Every private estate
which men claim by right presupposes a public condition
which they preserve by loyalty. An American is content, being
constrained, to defer to the public interest; he will submit to
paying an income tax if the pain of not paying is made greater
than the pain of submission. But your American typically refuses, in the pursuit of abstract commonwealth, to renounce

his personal claims to privacy. Without privacy there can be, in his reckoning, no commonwealth. He may moderate his private interest; he may be persuaded, for cause, to circumscribe it; but he steadfastly refuses to disown it, and upon this obdurate refusal is grounded his most revolutionary contribution to the idea of a democratic society. The private and the public interest are not in his political reflections inconsistent or opposed; in a right ordering of society they will be found to be, in fact, complementary and indivorcible; the object of all politics in America is to realize the one without extinguishing the other.

The possibility of conflict between the private and the public interest remains nevertheless, in American society, at all times open. Its presence is patently declared in the institution of collective bargaining which is designed to forestall it.

Labor relations in the private sector of the American industrial economy have been structured since 1935 by the National Labor Relations Act. The original piece of legislation, known as the Wagner Act, has been repeatedly amended in the interval since its enactment.[30] The essential thrust of the law remains. It confers upon workers in private industry the right to organize and bargain collectively, through representatives of their own choosing, concerning "wages, hours and other terms and conditions of employment." An employer's refusal to bargain in good faith may be cited as an "unfair labor practice" and enjoined by the act's enforcing agency, the National Labor Relations Board (NLRB).

The National Labor Relations Act is restricted to employer-employee relationships in the private sector. Its transforming influence was felt at once in factory, mine, and mill— in those centers where the great mass of industrial workers were congregated and where the efforts to organize were already, without benefit of encouragement by law, in old process. Some white-collar workers read the portents and were quick to respond to them. But it was not imagined that the new law was meant to apply to the faculties of private nonprofit educational institutions, and the NLRB at first declined to extend its jurisdiction to such cases. For more than three decades it hesitated at the threshold of the university. In 1951, asked to rule upon a petition brought in behalf of clerical employees of the libraries of Columbia University, the NLRB ruled that the relations of employees to an institution in which "the activities involved are noncommercial in nature and intimately connected with charitable and educational activities"[31] fell beyond its attentions. There the matter rested until in 1970 Cornell University, joined by Syracuse, appealed to the NLRB to reverse its decision. The service and maintenance employees of Syracuse were already organized under the rules of the New York State Labor Relations Board, and the two universities were simply announcing their preference, if they were obliged to bargain collectively with their nonacademic employees, to do so under the terms of federal law. In the case of Syracuse the NLRB refused to oppose itself to the New York State Labor Relations Board and dismissed the petition. For Cornell it ordered the election of a bargaining agent, acknowledging its awareness that in this exercise of discretion it was deliberately entering into "a hitherto uncharted area".[32]

The problematic implications of the decision were immediately felt. In a succession of cases—involving, first, Long Island University, and afterward Fordham and Adelphi[33]—the question at once arose whether the academic personnel of such institutions were to be regarded, in the NLRB's interpretation of the law, as "employees" or as "supervisors." Anyone could see that a president or a dean, whether or not he saw himself, or others saw him, as an academic, was at all events a supervisor, a person exercising the delegated authority of the governing board in hiring or firing, promoting or rewarding, disciplining or suspending, the workers in the vineyard.[34] But what was to be made of a department chairman or of a tenured professor, both of whom considered themselves, without pretense of rhetoric, party to the same delegation of duties, not merely enacting but framing and overseeing the roles of the university? Both were employees; both were at the same time responsible stewards of the free search for truth and its free exposition. Directly or indirectly, each performed positive tasks of supervision. If it was not quite true to say, exclusively, as Lionel Trilling said to Dwight D. Eisenhower, that the members of the faculty *were* the university, yet neither was it true to say that they were ordinary employees. The brief presented by Fordham University to the NLRB spoke for the community of scholars:

> The University has no existence independent of its faculty. It is the faculty which determines the character and quality of the University, and which effectively controls its academic policies and activities. The suggestion . . . that the faculty are merely "employees" of the University as a separate and distinct "employer" is a startling and unfounded distortion of the fundamental facts of university life. . . .

> The relationship among peers in a University's assemblage of scholars is *sui generis*. Any effort to analyze the University's assemblage in terms of an employer-employee relationship will necessarily distort the true state of affairs beyond recognition.[35]

The NLRB did not fail to hear the argument and in the Adelphi case even took pains to state it:

> The difficulty . . . may have potentially deep roots, stemming from the fact that the concept of collegiality, wherein power and authority is vested in a body composed of all one's peers or colleagues, does not square with the traditional authority structures with which this Act was designed to cope in the typical organizations of the commercial world. . . .

> Because authority vested in one's peers, acting as a group, simply would not conform to the pattern for which the supervisory exclusion of the Act was designed, a genuine system of collegiality would tend to confound us.[36]

The NLRB chose to resist anomaly and to doubt the genuineness of the system that produced it. The board preferred to see matters in terms of the adversarial relations to which it was by long habit accustomed. With respect to department chairmen, who were neither fish nor fowl, in whom the attributes of employer and employee were untidily conjoined, the NLRB tempered failure with casuistry and vacillated. But it admitted no doubts at last concerning the professors. Their "quasi-collegial authority" was an incident of employment, and the faculty were free, if they chose, to organize, to appoint a bargaining agent, and to bargain collectively concerning the terms and conditions of their labors.[37]

At Fordham, perplexed at the implications of this course of events, the law faculty filed a petition that it be permitted to bargain separately. No clearer demonstration of the distinction of tenure from job security could be adduced. With respect to private advantage, the separateness of the bargaining units made sense; with respect to the defense of academic freedom, it made none. On the contrary, the public interest that the university held in trust lapsed at once. The scholar's dedication to the free search for truth and its free exposition admits no division among faculties. In this, by consent to their single covenant, the faculties of the arts and sciences, of medicine and law, are all at one, cheek by jowl allied in one universe of inquiry and teaching. And that their alliance was at once forgotten is the strongest evidence of the decline of scholarship from its public commission in the American commonwealth.[38]

The force of the National Labor Relations Act does not run to public employees. Many public employments fall under the regulations of the Civil Service, and Congress had no intention of impairing its authority. In the eyes of public employees, however, the example of the success of organized labor in the private sector was disturbing. Not all employees on the public payrolls had civil service status, and even those who had it found in the system, in Mr. Garbarino's phrase, a too perfunctory "management of their discontent." The system reflected its origins. It primary motive was to protect the public against the erosive effects of the spoils system. It ministered to society's unquestionable solicitude for guaranteeing the continuity and maintaining the standards of government service. But as advocate of the interests of the government servant it had all of the parietal limitations of a company union. What did it matter that one's employer was the sovereign, if those employed to manage for the sovereign made the same errors, and needed the same corrections, as their counterparts in private industry? The Roman emperors on occasion allowed private persons to press claims that ran against the state. They proceeded on the maxim, *Legibus soluti legibus vivimus*, "We who are not bound by the law have nevertheless submitted to it". In the silence of law a democratic society could do no less. It must be ready to hear the reasonable demands of those nearest to it in commission. If the strike of policemen or firemen against the public service was unthinkable, the utility of a peaceful resolution of conflicts concerning fair terms and conditions of employment was not. The government could, without impairment of its proper authority, allow employees to organize and to bargain collectively within limits set by the public interest.

Such was the force and effect of a declaration of administrative policy—Executive Order 10988—issued by President Kennedy in 1962. President Nixon confirmed this pronouncement, with modifications, in Executive Order 11491 in 1969. The orders concur in conferring upon federal employees a right, a right limited but indefeasible, to bargain collectively in the federal system of employment. Government agencies and labor organizations that have been accorded exclusive recognition are directed, under the supervision of the Federal Labor Relations Council, "to meet . . . and confer in good faith with respect to personnel policies and practices and matters affecting working conditions."[39]

The new dispensation of the federal government was a signal for action in the states. Michigan and Massachusetts adopted comprehensive legislation in 1965, New York in 1967; today, forty states have such legislation, twenty-five of them legislation that extends the right of collective bargaining to employees in public higher education.

Of the massiveness of the transformation there can be no question. Two thirds of all faculty are in public institutions, and well over 100,000—more than a fifth of all full-time regular faculty—have allied themselves under the consent of law. The movement began in 1968 at the City University of New York. By 1980, some 681 institutions—among them such total sys-

tems as the State University of New York and the University
of Hawaii—had elected bargaining agents; 82 additional institutions, presented with the option, had in formal elections rejected it.[40]

5. ATHENA AND THE CYCLOPS

The suddenness of these developments, which now affected
the whole fabric of higher education, private as well as public,
struck consternation in all minds. In the AAUP it produced a
constitutional crisis. The officers of the Association were justly
puzzled. On campuses across the nation the American Feder-
ation of Teachers (AFT) and the National Education Association (NEA) were aggressively competing with each other for
the role of exclusive bargaining agent, and it was apprehended
that unless the AAUP followed the same pattern, its membership would scatter. The thing needed was a decision of principle, and it must be confessed that the members of the profession, anarchic by temperament, sorely divided in their
counsels, distracted by alarms, concerned with job security,
were lamentably unprepared to make it. They were accustomed to the slow processes of collegiality, and collegiality was
precisely the thing at stake. If a genuine system of collegiality
would tend to confound the NLRB, in such times it tended
also to confound those who were party to it, who had worked
immemorially in its terms, and who saw in it, not privatism,
not job security, not even the conquest of "shared authority,"
but the condition of public trust in the community of scholars.

The constitutional question that distressed the officers of
the Association was not, after all, whether collective bargaining was a useful pattern for advancing the profession. That
was a question about which the profession itself was divided,
and only experience could answer it. The question that needed
immediate resolution concerned the historic commission of
the AAUP, whether it could afford to be party to the disputes
it was called upon to arbitrate. Its historic commission, the
public commission that descended to it from the *Declaration of
1915*, was the reasoned defense of academic freedom, media-

torial, deliberative, critically detached, devoted to the resolution of conflicts by deference to principles of due process. If the AAUP chose to enter into competition for the role of bargaining agent, it could succeed only by disqualifying itself for the one role for which it was universally honored, for which it was distinctively equipped, and in which no other could take its place. Yet if, in order to remain a disinterested third party whose detachment was respected by all adversaries, it chose not to be one among them, it ran the risk of losing not only its influence but is membership as well.

The dilemma was clearly framed, and at the AAUP's Fifty-Eighth Annual Meeting the Association was asked to rule upon the position of its council:

The Association will pursue collective bargaining as a major additional way of realizing the Association's goals in higher education, and will allocate such resources and staff as are necessary for the vigorous selective development of this activity beyond present levels.[41]

The proposition was ratified by a margin of 7 to 1.

The Association is in error. William James used to tell of an unwed mother who sought to excuse the child in her belly on the ground that it was such a little one. The story needs recitation in all contemporary learned councils. The error of the Association lies, not in the little thing it has done, but in the great thing it has disqualified itself from doing. In competition with labor organizations it has asked to be recognized in the role of exclusive bargaining agent. The law allows but one such agent in any bargaining unit and forbids employers, once an agent has been chosen, to have any dealings with its rivals. Therefore, the mediatorial function of the AAUP—its major traditional role as disinterested third party, as guarantor of due process, as defender of the covenant of free scholarship—this role, upon which its historic commission is based, has been vacated. On every organized campus the AAUP is disqualified for the role of mediator, by interest wherever it is the bargaining agent, by legal exclusion wherever it is not.

The demand for mediation remains; even on organized campuses it remains; and if the AAUP is unable or unwilling to answer to this demand, another must be found to answer in its place. In the structure of American higher education, if the AAUP did not exist, it would be necessary to invent it.

In a dissenting opinion—it is one of the finest briefs in the distinguished literature of the Association—precisely this was affirmed. Sanford H. Kadish, William W. Van Alstyne, and Robert K. Webb wrote: "Our record of extended influence in shaping the norms of higher education for several generations has derived . . . from our reasoned appeal to common commitment and moral legitimacy rather than the play of power in adversary relationships."[42]

The question of collegiality was after all, for all scholars, the nub of the argument. In the secrecy of their closets not even the partisans of collective bargaining were disposed to doubt it, and every effort was made to persuade the loyal opposition among their colleagues that the free search for truth and its free exposition, which was their common interest and society's trust delegated to their care, could be handled in a contract. The subject of their division from each other (so it was argued) was a matter of form, not of substance; tenure was but job security; and as one negotiated wages and hours and the terms and conditions of employment, so also one could negotiate the security of the scholar in the public life.

But the security of the scholar in the public life is not ours to negotiate. The administration of a university—of Harvard or Chicago, of Michigan or California—cannot confer it. Only the public has the power to confer it, and the public confers it always in its own interest, always to satisfy its need for open discussion and the free exchange of ideas. Tenure is a trusteeship, not a privatism. To treat it as an incident of private employment, as a stratagem of clerks or the conspiracy of a profession, is to condemn it.

That is why we need indispensably to restore the paradigm of the tenure of the judge in public office. Why do we shield the justices of the Supreme Court, during good behavior, with the immunities of tenure? Not to satisfy them but to satisfy ourselves. We interest ourselves not in the permanence of their jobs but in the uncompromised independence of their opinions. Burdened fiduciaries of the public interest, they labor to discover the vector of our covenant. Therefore, necessarily, we put them beyond our contests, beyond all of the adversary relationships that attend our ordinary private encounters. Our confidence in their detachment must not be marred by the suspicion that considerations of private interest have colored their conduct of the public business. The tenure of the judge in public office is the formal condition of the rule of law in human society. It will not guarantee the rule of law. But without it there can be no rule of law, nor any private freedom, theirs or ours, under it.

The tenure of scholars rests upon the same premises. It has but one object, to put the pursuit of knowledge beyond our partisan contests, beyond all of the adversary relationships of our ordinary private exchanges. Therefore, tenure is not subject to negotiation as wages and hours are subject to it, or as the terms and conditions of employment are subject to it. Scholars have as personal a concern with the terms of their employment as any other breed of laborers. But they acknowledge a duty of detachment that belongs only to them, and no pattern of bargaining, individual or collective, can be permitted to take its place, or to substitute for it, or to jeopardize it, in the public understanding. The public demands, as a condition of service to itself, that the free search for truth be immunized from considerations of private interest that would qualify it, or color it, or compromise its public character. Society can and always will withhold any merely professional privilege that cannot be shown to make a moral claim upon it. The university wears its moral authority by virtue of such a claim, and it is a miseducation of the public to confound this claim with a private interest of the scholar in his own security.

NOTES

1. *U.S. Constitution,* article II, section 2.
2. Ibid., section 4.
3. Ibid., article III, section 1. The old phrase is: *Quamdiu bene se gesserint.*
4. *McCulloch* v. *Maryland,* 4 Wheaton 316, at 415 (1819).

5. *Osborn* v. *U.S. Bank*, 9 Wheaton 738, at 866 (1824).

6. Cf. *Immanuel Kant's Critique of Pure Reason*, translated by Norman Kemp Smith (London: Macmillan, 1929), pp. 210–211, 218–233.

7. *McCulloch* v. *Maryland*, 4 Wheaton 316, at 421. See also 415.

8. Cf. Edward S. Corwin, *The Constitution and What It Means Today* (New York: Atheneum, 1967 [1920]), pp. 135–136.

9. Fritz Machlup, "In Defense of Academic Tenure," 50 *AAUP Bulletin* (Summer 1964): 112–124, at 119.

10. Clark Byse and Louis Joughin, *Tenure in American Higher Education: Plans, Practices, and the Law* (Ithaca, N.Y.: Cornell University Press, 1959), p. 4.

11. *Academic Freedom and Tenure, A Handbook of the American Association of University Professors*, edited by Louis Joughin (Madison: University of Wisconsin Press, 1969 [1967]), pp. 33–39. Hereafter referred to as *AAUP Handbook*.

12. Ibid., pp. 155–176.

13. The list includes, among others, the Association of American Law Schools, the American Political Science Association, the Association for Higher Education, the National Education Association, the American Philosophical Association, the American Psychological Association, the American Historical Association, the Modern Language Association of America, the American Economic Association, the American Council of Learned Societies, the American Sociological Association, the Association of State Colleges and Universities, the American Mathematical Society, the John Dewey Society for the Study of Education and Culture, the United Chapters of Phi Beta Kappa.

14. *AAUP Handbook*, p. 34.

15. Fritz Machlup has written contrarily (op. cit., p. 179): "Academic freedom antedates general freedom of speech by several hundreds of years, and its development was quite separate and independent. In the United States, academic freedom is not a right that professors or students have under the Constitution or under any law of the land, whereas general freedom of speech is one of the civil liberties protected by the Bill of Rights in our Constitution. While violations of this right can be taken to the courts of law, infringements of academic freedom can be protected only by appealing to the conscience of individuals and groups in society; there is no recourse to the courts except where contractual relations are involved."

Historically, in point of development, the separateness of the two notions—academic freedom and general freedom of speech—is demonstrable; their logical independence is not. This is precisely the significance, in our century, of the Supreme Court's decisions concerning academic freedom under the First and Fourteenth Amendments. See, above, chapter III. The development at law is incomplete; but the two traditions have been conjoined, and the implication of the one in the other affirmed, in the Court's interpretation.

16. Preamble of the *Constitution of the United States*. Cf. Corwin, op. cit., p. 2: "As a *document* the Constitution came from the generation of 1787; as a *law* it derives its force and effect from the present generation of American citizens, and hence should be interpreted in the light of present conditions and with a view to meeting present problems."

17. *AAUP Handbook*, pp. 34–35.

18. Cf. Sanford H. Kadish, "The Strike and the Professoriat," in *Dimensions of Academic Freedom* (Urbana: University of Illinois Press, 1969), pp. 44–45.

19. *Faculty Tenure, A Report and Recommendations by the Commission on Academic Tenure in Higher Education (William R. Keast, Chairman)* (San Francisco: Jossey-Bass Publishers, 1973), pp. 1–20. Hereafter referred to as *Report of the Keast Commission*. See also Byse and Joughin, op. cit., pp. 9–70.

20. Cf. "Discussion Memorandum on Academic Tenure at Harvard University," issued in November 1971 by Harvard's University Committee on Governance and reproduced (in part) in 58 *AAUP Bulletin* (Spring 1972): 62–68, at 62: " 'Academic tenure' means simply the contingent right of a faculty member appointed to a tenure position to retain that position ['"without periodic reappointment"'] until retirement."

Machlup, op. cit., *AAUP Handbook*, pp. 306–338, at pp. 310–311: "Let us then define academic tenure as the 'title' . . . or . . . ground on which the teacher or investigator may confidently expect to hold his position until he is retired for age or permanent disability or separated for adequate cause under due process or because of financial exigencies of the institution."

Byse and Joughin, op. cit., p. 2: ". . . the essential characteristic of tenure . . . is continuity of service, in that the institution in which the teacher serves has in some manner—either as a legal obligation or as a moral commitment—relinquished the freedom or power it otherwise would possess to terminate the teacher's services."

Report of the Keast Commission, p. 256: "*Academic Tenure*—an arrangement under which faculty appointments in an institution of higher education are continued until retirement for age or physical disability, subject to dismissal for adequate cause or unavoidable termination on account of financial exigency or change of institutional program."

21. *AAUP Handbook*, pp. 36–37.

22. The AAUP's original statement of principles—the *Declaration of 1915*—prescribes a maximum of ten years, but no required minimum. The *Report of the Keast Commission* recommends a maximum of seven years, a minimum of "not less than five years" (p. 65).

23. *AAUP Handbook*, p. 37.

24. *Report of the Keast Commission*, pp. 5, 65.

25. Cf. the American Association of University Professors' policy document "Academic Freedom and Tenure in the Quest for National Security" in 42 *AAUP Bulletin* (Spring 1956): 61: "No opportunity for hearing is normally required in connection with failure to reappoint. If, however, there are reasonable grounds to believe that a nontenured staff member was denied reappointment for reasons that violate academic freedom, there should be a hearing before a faculty committee. In such a hearing the burden of proof is on the persons who assert that there were improper reasons for the failure to reappoint." Again, in the AAUP's "1968 Recommended Institutional Regulations on Academic Freedom and Tenure" (54 *AAUP Bulletin* [Winter 1968]: 451–452), it is provided: "The burden of proof shall rest with [the complainant]. If he succeeds in establishing a prima facie case, it is incumbent upon those who made the decision not to reappoint him to come forward with evidence in support of their decision." Cf. William Van Alstyne, "Tenure: A Summary, Explanation, and 'Defense,' " 58 *AAUP Bulletin* (Autumn 1971): 328–333.

Under the due process clause of the Fourteenth Amendment, a nontenured person in a public institution has no right to a statement of reasons for nonrenewal or to a formal hearing, unless it can be shown that, in the absence of these, he is deprived of a "liberty" (e.g., the opportunity of seeking employment elsewhere without stigma) or a "property interest" (e.g., an acquisition of *de facto* tenure under the rules and practices of the employing institution): *Board of Regents of State Colleges* v. *David F. Roth*, 408 U.S. 564 (1972); *Charles R. Perry* v. *Robert P. Sindermann*, 408 U.S. 593 (1972).

26. *AAUP Handbook*, p. 175: "In every institution the grounds which will be regarded as justifying the dismissal of members of the faculty should be formulated with reasonable definiteness."

27. *Statement of Policy on Appointment and Tenure at Stanford University, January 9, 1973*, II, 1. Cf. *Report of the Keast Commission*, 75, p. 256: "(a) demonstrated incompetence or dishonesty in teaching or research, (b) substantial and manifest neglect of duty, and (c) personal conduct which substantially impairs the individual's fulfillment of his institutional responsibilities."

28. *Report of the Keast Commission*, pp. 89–90. Cf. *Report of the*

Special Committee on Campus Tensions, S. M. Linowitz, Chairman (Washington, D.C.: American Council on Education, 1970), p. 42: "The justification for tenure is the crucial protection it gives to academic freedom. Professors who espouse unpopular views must be free from reprisal. Tenure was not devised in the spirit of trade union systems to guarantee job security. But it has come to serve this function too, at a cost."

29. One of the superstitions of the labor movement is that the race of laborers is richer, that it takes to itself a larger share of the national income, by reason of organization. Theodore J. St. Antoine, Dean of the University of Michigan Law School, has written:

"If the experience of industrial unionization is any indicator, such organization will not bring about the substantial economic change that many faculty members undoubtedly hope for. Labor economists are convinced that unionization has not substantially changed the proportion of corporate income going to wage earners. That conclusion is verified in many different industries throughout the past seventy years. . . . the working force is getting approximately the same proportion it would have received in the absence of unionization, i.e., approximately 65 to 70 percent.

"Certainly unions have not been without economic effect. The most noticeable change they have produced has been an average increase of 10 to 15 percent in rates of pay—a change employers have promptly offset by reducing the number of employees through more efficient production techniques. Productivity improvements, not unionization, are directly responsible for the overall increase in the real wages of working people." *Faculty Power: Collective Bargaining on Campus*, edited by Terrence N. Tice (Ann Arbor, Mich.: The Institute of Continuing Legal Education, 1972), p. 2. Cf. H. G. Lewis, *Unionism and Relative Wages in the United States* (Chicago: University of Chicago Press, 1963), pp. 4–5, 9, 193.

This conclusion will not decide the question, whether collective bargaining is desirable as a device for gaining the ends of the community of scholars; but it puts to rest one of the spurious claims that are ordinarily made in support of it. The unions minister to the interests of the tenured, not of the untenured.

30. The Fair Labor Standards Act (1938), Taft-Hartley (1947), and Landrum-Griffin (1959) amend it; administrative rulings and court decisions qualify its application in use. Cf. Derek C. Bok and John T. Dunlop, *Labor and the American Community* (New York: Simon and Schuster, 1970). The sections of the act (as amended) that treat collective bargaining appear in 29 United States Code 151–168 (1970).

31. *Trustees of Columbia University*, 97 NLRB 424, 427 (1951).

32. *The Cornell Case,* 183 *NLRB* 41 (1970).

33. *Fordham University,* 193 *NLRB* 23 (1971); *C. W. Post Center* (Long Island University), 189 *NLRB* 109 (1971); *Brooklyn Center* (Long Island University), 189 *NLRB* 110 (1971); *Adelphi University,* 195 *NLRB* 107 (1972).

34. For the definition of "supervisor" see NLRA 2 (11), 29 United States Code 152 (11).

35. *Brief of Fordham University,* pp. 8, 74. Quoted in Robert K. Carr and Daniel K. Van Eyck, *Collective Bargaining Comes to the Campus* (Washington, D.C.: American Council on Education, 1973), p. 32.

36. Quoted in Carr and Van Eyck, op. cit., p. 34.

37. The issue is not yet closed. In February 1979 the Supreme Court agreed to review a decision of the U.S. Court of Appeals for the Second Circuit (New York). In *National Labor Relations Board* v. *Yeshiva University* (No. 77-4182, July 31, 1978, Ref. 98 LRRM 3245), the Appeals Court, restricting itself "solely to the situation of the institution involved in this proceeding," had ruled that full-time faculty members at Yeshiva University exercise "supervisory and managerial functions" and are therefore not subject to the provisions of the National Labor Relations Act.

In February 1980, in a 5 to 4 decision, the Supreme Court had affirmed the decision of the Appeals Court. The opinion (No. 78-857) is printed in *The Chronicle of Higher Education* 19, no. 23 (February 25, 1980), pp. 7–9. The decision applies specifically only to Yeshiva University. But in the measure that Yeshiva's administrative structure is regarded as typical, the stability of some eighty collective bargaining agreements at private institutions is threatened, and the possibility arises that collective bargaining may not extend beyond private colleges and universities with existing contracts. (The decision has no bearing on the status of faculty unions at publicly supported institutions.)

38. Fordham University has twice rejected collective bargaining in less than two years. As of May 31, 1976, only its law faculty was organized.

39. Executive Order No. 11491, 3 C.F.R. 191, sec. 11a (1969 Comp.). President Kennedy's Executive Order No. 10988 appears in 3 C.F.R. 521 (1959–1963 Comp.).

40. *The Chronicle of Higher Education* (July 7, 1980), pp. 7–8.

41. 59 *AAUP Bulletin* (1973): 146.

42. "The Manifest Unwisdom of the AAUP as a Collective Bargaining Agent," 58 *AAUP Bulletin,* 57–61, at 58. By 1979 collective bargaining was absorbing more than 25 percent of the Association's

$2.2 million budget. Of 633 institutions that had elected bargaining agents, only 56 had chosen to be represented by the AAUP. Membership in the association had dwindled to 56,000 from a high of 78,000. *New York Times*, June 23, 1980, p. A14.

6.

EDUCATION, THE UNIVERSITY, AND THE SOCIAL COVENANT

The community of scholars is its own first problem. But it is as ill equipped in its modern pattern to understand its own community as to understand the community of the market or the nation or the union of nations beyond it. Our pattern ignores the structure of peace in any of its forms—in inquiry, in exchange, in politics, in discourse, in religion, or in art. We are Icarus with the problems of Daedalus. Therefore, on questions of education, in this and the next chapter I must ask for a patience that is suited to the gravity of our enterprise. In what I am about to say, I shall in fact be laying down a criticism of the foundations of the social sciences. That is the very thing needed, an understanding of the terms of social analysis that are essential if the sciences and humanities are to be brought together, and their contributions reconciled, in the education of our young. The university is itself, however, too specialized a form of society to serve as the paradigm of social analysis. Therefore, let me make the argument first in relation to the clearer case of the idea of a science of politics. I shall then have prepared the way for a theory of higher education suited to our season.

1. QUESTIONS OF PATH

In any serious reflection upon the social condition of human beings we raise, typically, two kinds of questions. The first kind I describe as *Questions of Path;* the second, as *Questions of Covenant.* Questions of Path and Questions of Covenant correspond to two distinct orders of obligation. Therefore, in the conduct of a science of political relations, it is indispensable to distinguish the two kinds of questions that will inevitably arise.

At the beginning of the seventeenth century, Francis Bacon meditated the foundations of a new science. He wrote in *The Great Instauration:*

Man is but the servant and interpreter of nature: what he does and what he knows is only what he has observed of nature's order in fact or in thought; beyond this he knows nothing and can do nothing.

For the chain of causes cannot by any force be loosed or broken, nor can nature be commanded except by being obeyed.[1]

The passage is prophetic. In Bacon's day it was revolutionary. It proclaimed a reformation of the sciences as radical in its way as that other Reformation that even at that moment, in blood and riot and iconoclasm, was disturbing the religious fabric of all Europe. Bacon was announcing the program as well as the motive of the sciences we nowadays describe as "empirical," that is, of all of the sciences of behavior that ground themselves, as a point of method, on the evidences of experience. For more than three hundred years the behavioral sciences have challenged the best energies, and exercised the most exalted intellects, of Western society. Taken together, they represent all that we mean by "science" in the narrow sense of the term that has become customary in our language. Wherever men speak of the conquest of nature in the modern world, they intend to refer to that understanding of the uniformity of nature that is realized in the modern sciences of behavior.

The behavioral sciences are concerned exclusively with Questions of Path.

Questions of Path are questions concerning the limits which nature lays upon our acts. Those limits define, in relation to our purposes and initiatives as actors in the world, the domain of real possibility. They are the study and last object of all technology, of the applied part of all of our accomplished sciences. Our positive sciences of nature and society are all without exception attempts to understand in theory the uniform patterns of behavior which, being known, will enable us to predict the natural consequences of our acts. That capacity for prediction which the sciences confer upon us has, in relation to the conduct of our lives, the most extraordinary practical utility. For if, quite independently of our desires or aversions, we know that wherever a certain set of conditions is produced, a certain result may be confidently expected to follow—as that when a stone is exposed to the light of the sun, it will absorb heat, or when a cherry pit is planted in the soil, under specifiable conditions of warmth and moisture a tree will grow—if, I say, we know these patterns, namely, the causal conditions of effects in nature, we have then the power to produce those effects, or to avoid them, according to our interest. To produce those effects is to supply the natural conditions of their emergence; to avoid those effects is to prevent the natural conditions of their emergence.

Suppose that we possessed a perfected science of psychology, a psychology so perfectly evolved as to instruct us concerning the necessary and sufficient conditions of learning. A knowledge of the conditions that are conjointly necessary if learning is to take place in a child would confer upon us an extraordinary power, the power (other things being equal) to produce learning wherever we intended it. We should have, in perfect strictness of language, a method of teaching, the knowledge of the path that would enable us to gain, with critical understanding, the results we seek after.

"Whoever wills the end . . . ," says the philosopher Kant, "wills also the indispensably necessary means to it that lie in his power."[2] It is well said, and it is one of the great and arresting reflections of philosophy on the finitude of the human condition how little at last lies within our power. What is in our power? Never the path, but only the taking of it. The path belongs to nature; to us belongs only the decision, which concerns ourselves, whether we are content to walk it. We act for our interests and for their sake only, but nature preserves its own order, sublimely careless of our presence, its brute course undeflected by the desires and aversions we bring to it. Such freedom as we have in the pursuit of our interests is always a freedom under nature's conditions, for we remain equally subject to its conditions, whether we walk in knowledge or ignorance, in efficiency or futility, in affluence or want.

That is why in all conduct there is an element of art. The artist is, like all of us, a pensioner of nature. A sculptor works with borrowed materials, with clay or stone or bronze, materials that have their own properties, their own inherent limitations or possibilities, quite independently of his act. The object of his art is to make those materials respond to what he wants of them. But what he wants is not necessarily, and is never wholly, what he is prepared to get. What he is prepared to get is fatefully circumscribed. For he can have only what the medium can equally afford; beyond that he can have nothing. In all that he produces he is governed absolutely by the limits of the medium in which he works. Within those limits he is free, free to choose his path, free to create a world in his own image; but beyond those limits, which are set intransigently by the medium he has chosen, he is forbidden to pass.

Just so, in the conduct of an industrial economy, we extract by labor and allocate by design the resources that nature impassively affords without our labor and without design. But in all of this heroic expenditure of effort we have added not a single utility to nature's stock. The ore above the soil is the same as the ore beneath it. Transportation has not increased its utility; it has simply readied it for use, placed it where the need for it is felt, supplied it where its utility may be exploited. All that economy can ever achieve is this redistribution of utilities that it has simply found. Their quantity in nature remains, after allocation as before it, fixed. For it is not nature, but ourselves, that economy serves. When an economist allocates scarce resources with a view to maximizing utility, he leaves the measure of utility untouched. What in fact he maximizes is not utility but our power to draw upon it. The wealth of nature is without increase; but the wealth of nations is by design made greater than it was.

Questions of Path are, in a word, questions of utility, of what is in fact useful in connection with our purposes. *If I would gain an end, what ought I to do?* That is the form of the whole class of questions I describe as Questions of Path. The answer to a Question of Path will always be given in the form of an imperative. You would gain an end? Provide then the means that are in fact essential to the having of it. The end is an effect wanted; the imperative stipulates an obligation to perform those acts that will produce the natural conditions of its emergence.

A Question of Path is a question of fact, not of morals. The goodness or badness of the ends we pursue is not at issue. The question concerns itself only with the relative utility of the means at our disposal. It is a question, not of moral, but of technical rightness, of what I shall call *material* as distinct from *moral* obligation. In our ordinary phrasing, it concerns efficiency, and where such a question concerning efficiency is asked, at least wherever it is asked and understood, the answer must be sought, in the sleep of all conscience, in the moral silence of nature. There is, after all, as Clarence Irving Lewis once tartly observed, a *right* way to repair a jukebox.

The example is, I sincerely hope, perfectly conclusive. There are in nature paths to evil as well as paths to good, straight paths to Sodom as well as crooked paths to Jerusalem; and if it behooves us in our moral adventure to know our last goals, it behooves us also and equally to know the paths upon which we may act for their sake. I may perhaps, out of my soul's surmise, claim to arbitrate the goodness of the goal. It is good because it interests me, or good because I count it good, or good because I desire it. But the rightness of the path is not determined by the goodness of the goal or by the circumstance that I pursue it. The rightness of the path is a fact of the world and must be determined, as we determine other matters of fact, by observation of nature's unarguable habit. That is why we discover such infinite pathos in those words of poor Othello at his journey's end. He meditates the sleeping Desdemona (he is about to murder her):

When I have pluckt the rose,
I cannot give it vital growth again,
It needs must wither. . . .

His purpose is grounded in a lie; his goal is infamous; his path is exquisite and fatal.

2. QUESTIONS OF COVENANT

Niccolò Machiavelli is by general consent accounted the father of political science, and it is in fact instructive, in assessing pedigrees, to inquire with what justice he is assigned the honor of paternity. He was by no means the first to reflect upon man's political condition. Plato, Aristotle, and the Stoics, Cicero and the Roman lawyers, Saint Augustine, Saint Thomas Aquinas, and even Dante had labored before him. All alike had labored as strenuously, and some surely with an immeasurably superior genius, to understand our political covenants, the grounds of legal obligation, the nature of the good society, and the objects of government. Germinal, majestic, profound, their conceptions formed at the beginning of the sixteenth

century, they form still today, the great background of political
reflection in the West, against which all modern ideas of political community must be seen in order to be understood. And
of the giants in the earth who came after Machiavelli—of
Hobbes, Locke and Montesquieu, of Rousseau, Hegel and
Marx—not one was content to be his son. Why, then, should
Machiavelli, this wild olive grafted onto an ancient stock, be
accounted the root of a tree of which he is so palpably a
branch and minor offshoot?

The reason is already before us. Machiavelli is not the first
political philosopher; he is simply the first philosopher who
was able to see, in the raw struggle for power that is the actuality of our political experience, the domain of an empirical
science.

Machiavelli's proper achievement lies in a radical decision
of method, to limit political reflection to what we have been
attempting to distinguish as Questions of Path. He performed
for the study of politics the same role which Bacon performed
for the study of nature at large. He challenged men to the pursuit of a new science of behavior, a momentous and tragically
consequent new science, which took seriously, for once, the
real possibilities of the City of Man. Such a science was to be
acquired, not by speculation on the objects of government or
the aims of God, but by observation of the actualities of power
in the brute arena where power is exercised and contested,
and the game won or lost, according to calculable patterns that
experience makes cleanly visible. He proposed to examine political reality, political reality rid of all political illusion and
moral chicane and rhetoric. He was the first philosopher who
worked while God rested. And there can be no question that
of all of the philosophers of the great tradition he would have
been most at home in the inner councils where decisions are
made, behind closed doors, at an American Watergate.

Machiavelli chose by a deliberate abstraction, in the study
of political power, to suspend judgment on its social commissions. The study of politics is thus restricted to the study of

the observable conditions under which the power of government is made effective in the life of any society. It is simply
the study of human ecology, a study of the ecological relationships subsisting among partisan groups in the human environment. Just as, in the life of the desert, given the powers of
the species that inhabit there, given the powers of hawk,
snake, and rodent, of cactus, salt-grass, and tumbleweed,
there is a natural equilibrium to which those powers will gravitate, and in which, once realized, there is no further tendency
to change, so, in the body politic, given the powers that are
loosed within it, there is a *natural* equilibrium to which they
will gravitate. Combinations, leagues, and alliances may vary;
but if the equilibrium is stable, the power of one group or of
a combination of groups will invariably preponderate. That
power is what Machiavelli intends by government. As power
is redistributed, the government will change. But for any distribution of power an equilibrium is predictable, and the topic
of political science is the set of causal conditions by which that
equilibrium is achieved.

If the prospect of such knowledge must excite princes in
the ignorant caucus where there is no competent authority to
impeach it, then how much more shall it excite academics in
the ignorant closet where there is no competent theory to
question its adequacy, to qualify its claims, or to remind men
of the abstraction by which it has been gained?

Admit legitimacy to lie where the power of command lies,
suspend the distinction between force and authority, we may
have a positive science of politics, a science grounded in experience and confirmed by observation, established beyond all
caprice of opinion and all fugitive human conventions in the
paths of nature itself. In short, if we will be content to ask
Questions of Path and to set aside all questions concerning the
terms under which men will consent voluntarily, of their own
motion, to submit to government, we may acquire all of the
instruments for commanding men that now already we possess for commanding other parcels of nature. We shall have a

natural science of politics, sufficient to the task of answering the primordial question of all actual governments, namely, how to gain power and how, having gained it, to keep it.

What has been left out, excluded by systematic omission, in order to arrive at this new science? The answer of political philosophy is that Machiavelli has deliberately excluded from the purview of his science all Questions of Covenant.

Questions of Path are questions concerning the limits which nature lays upon our acts. Questions of Covenant are, on the contrary, questions concerning the limits which we lay upon ourselves. Their topic is not nature but man, not material but moral obligation.

Questions of Covenant are the province and inciting occasion of the whole range of the historical sciences. They are the prime questions we confront in any informed study of the "humanities." For the things studied in the humanities—the restraints of law and politics, the imperatives of religion and economy, all of the profound obligations of art and language and logic—all of these are covenants self-imposed. They are conditions of our moral community with each other. Whether we would have moral community with one another, we are free to choose. But if we would have it, we are then no longer free to trifle with the conditions of civility that are essential to the achievement of it. These conditions are not natural; yet neither are they arbitrary. And that is what we moderns have to understand. It remains for us to discover out of tragic debacle, out of the unintermitted ruin of our century, that there are objective conditions of peace just as there are objective conditions of war.

In the seventeenth century, in a book that bore the sinister and forbidding title of *Leviathan,* the philosopher Hobbes undertook to make a distinction between two conditions of men—the condition of men in a civil order of society and the condition of men in what he chose to describe as a "state of nature."

By the state of nature Hobbes intended to indicate what the human situation would be if the rule of law were to be at one stroke suspended in the relations of men to one another. The prospect scandalizes the imagination. For the effect would be to destroy on the part of every man the capacity to frame normal expectations of any other. Every art of civilization would be suspended, every vestige of property erased, and the lives of men would become "solitary, poor, nasty, brutish and short," in a collision of egotisms which Hobbes described as a *bellum omnium contra omnes* ("a war of all against all").

When it was suggested to Hobbes that this condition was a fiction nowhere to be found in any historical society, he replied with a shrug that the state of nature is the characteristic phenomenon witnessed in every season of the world in the relations of nation-states to each other. Balances of power they have; peace they have not; and the nation that mistakes the one for the other shall do so at its own peril.

The nations of the earth stand opposite to each other in the moral silence of nature. Each professes a sovereignty unabridged save as it consents to lay abridgments on itself. Therefore, in the absence of any rule of law acknowledged by all parties to the competition, every power must appear arbitrary, and every concert of powers a raw accident of nature. The distinction between power proper and power improper, between authority and force, can have no incidence in such a scene. That precisely is the absolute terribleness of the state of nature: that no nation that is party to the natural equilibrium can govern it; that every nation is subject to it; and that, in the absence of any rule of law commonly admitted, by which the nations are content to civilize their contests with one another, it becomes the insensate condemnation of us all.

The institution of covenants arises from the need, whether of men or of nations, to establish an order of normal expectations that none of the parties to the covenant is able to achieve, or to guarantee, privately and unilaterally.

Hobbes used to say: "Covenants without the sword are but words, and of no strength to secure a man at all."[3] And it may, in the political rubble of our century, be so. Yet it does not follow, and the moral havoc of our time forbids us to assume, that the sword without a covenant is a civility. It is not. Civility is the condition of peace under law that we have authorized, and no sword, no force in nature, can authorize it for us.

It is not the business of social analysis to decide for mankind whether mankind wants civilization. But analysis can show, if mankind wants it, the terms of consent that are essential to the achievement of it, the terms that are prerequisite, in every domain of human activity, to the establishment of normal expectations among men, whether in a legal order, or a community of exchange, or a church, or a universe of inquiry, or a language. These conditions—conditions of politics and the market, of religion and science, of art and communication—are precisely the part of the human world which nature unassisted fails to afford. They are the part of our world which in the effort to achieve community we are compelled to institute, voluntarily putting ourselves under covenants with one another according to our last partisanships.

3. THE FOUNDATIONS OF MORAL COMMUNITY

Immanuel Kant used to declare that two things excited his soul, the starry heavens above and the moral law within. The modern mentality shares his wonder, and has even studied to extend his wonder, before the first of these. There is no danger that a human being, born into the twentieth century, will take lightly the illimitable fact of the starry heavens above. But that same human being, if he has not learned to repudiate belief in the moral law within, has become nevertheless profoundly suspicious of it. He is apt to see in any profession of moral law in human affairs simply another poor profession of the time-entangled human soul, a piece of ideology inherited by historical accident and perpetuated by animal sloth. Kant thought otherwise. He formulated the moral law, or, as he called it, "the categorical imperative," in the following:

Act so that you treat humanity, whether in your own person or in that of another, always as an end and never as a means only.[4]

It is important for all students of political obligation, in spite of fashionable opinion, to meditate that sentence. The question is not whether it was written by Kepler's geometer God but what its meaning is. What does it *mean* to treat another human being, or for that matter oneself, "always as an end and never as a means only"? In any attempt to understand the meaning of that imperative it will be found indispensably necessary to mark a distinction between *things* and *persons*. Technically, the terms belong to jurisprudence. But the distinction itself is coeval with the phenomenon of human community in any of its forms. It is profoundly the most fundamental distinction of human social theory, and I know of no path to it which is either so direct or for present purposes so instructive as the little treatise of the late Martin Buber, entitled *I and Thou*.[5]

Any two objects that I perceive in the order of nature stand related to each other as thing to thing. Let any relation that runs between things in nature be described, in Buber's phrasing, as an "It-It" relation. Such a relation is discovered, for instance, between this sheet of paper and the table on which it lies. And the same kind of relation is exhibited when an external observer contemplates the relation of light rays reflected from the paper to the retina of my eye. He considers an "It-It" relation, a relation of things interconnected in the system of nature. My retina, no less than the paper and the light rays, is an "It" in that system. It is a physical body implicated in the same physical transaction in which the paper and the light rays are implicated, and nothing in its physical estate is altered or qualified by the circumstance that it is mine.

The external observer who studies the reflection of the light rays to my eye is of course also a denizen of nature. He, too, is caught up in that order. But he does not for the purposes of his study consider himself party to the physical transaction he observes. He regards himself as a neutralized observer, the deliberately detached spectator of nature's order, which would remain the same even if it were unobserved. He, therefore, as he will represent his own performance, figures in a different kind of relation, in a relation Buber would describe as an "I-It" relation. The observer encounters a complex transaction in nature. Let him be described as the "subject" of the encounter, and let the transaction he observes, namely, the light rays reflected from the paper to the retina of my eye, be described as the "object" of the encounter. The subject is a person perceiving, the object an array of things perceived; and the subject stands related in that encounter no longer merely as "It" to "It" but as a detached observer of the order of things observed, as "I" to "It."

Different from either of these relations is the relation in which we stand, you and I, in our present encounter with each other in this discourse. For this relationship, though we do not see each other's faces (and even if we did), is a relation not of thing to thing or of person to thing, but of person to person.

Mark the difference, since everything I have to say depends upon the discrimination of this difference. The matter in question is not a matter of ideology but of perspective. I who speak stand related to you who attend, at least for this occasion, to what I say. We are for this interval party to a common undertaking. We constitute by mutual consent or forbearance a miniature society, a temporary community of inquiry, and I speak for the sake of communicating with you, in order to advance our shared concern.

Therefore, to that end, I as subject address you as also subject concerning matters that are the objects of our study. I so order my language that it may serve as a shared idiom, linking my reflections to yours. I enact an implicit dialogue. I in speaking put myself into the role of yourself in hearing, in order that, according to the mutually observed conventions of our common language, we may not merely speak and hear but also understand in common. We stand related as parties to a common discourse, both alike as subjects entered into a common implicit covenant (in this instance, a mutually shared set of conventions of language and a mutually shared set of rules governing the admission of evidence and the meaning of proof) for the exchange of our thoughts. We stand opposite to each other, not as object to object, nor as subject to object, but as subject to subject, as *dramatis personae*, persons party to a community of inquiry, in what Buber describes, without sentiment or metaphor, as an "I-Thou" relationship.

This kind of relationship, this relationship of persons who consent in mutuality to a common covenant, is our creative achievement in the moral silence of nature, and this kind of achievement is the very topic to which all study of human institutions, distinctively so called, is ultimately addressed.

I do not attempt to demonstrate the presence of "I-Thou" relations in our lives, or even to raise the question whether human community is ever perfectly realized. In our simple encounters of every day, the fact is that in some connections we have it, in others we do not. But the actual order or disarray of our lives is not, after all, in question. The only serious question is: If human beings want community (wherever they want it and whenever they want it), what are the terms upon which alone they may have it? And that is precisely the sense of Kant's moral imperative: "Act so that you treat humanity, whether in your own person or in that of another, always as an end and never as a means only." He who stands within my moral community I am obliged to treat as a *person*, that is to say (if I may now appropriate the meaning of the term in jurisprudence), as a *subject of rights*, a "Thou," whose claim to dignity is essential to my own. He who stands beyond my moral community I am free to treat as a mere *thing*, that is to say, as an *object* in nature, an "It," that may be arbitrarily used without respect for rights and without restraint upon my action.

That a human being is obliged to be his brother's keeper is never really questioned by anyone. That is the rudimentary demand of any community whatever, and not even Hobbes questions it. The parties to a community are related to each other otherwise than they are related to those who fall beyond their number. That is why, as they see themselves, their community is in nature but never of it. As they see themselves (however others see them), there is never any question whether the community shall be set apart. The community must be set apart. Cain is inevitably his brother's keeper. The only real question is: Who is his brother? Who belongs to the community, and who does not? Who is member, and who is alien? For if, in the society that Cain is willing to affirm, only Cain is member, he wanders desolate, thing among things, beyond civility in the state of nature, through all the world.

Who is my brother? With respect to that question, in the political life of any society, an authentic science of politics must be able to supply an answer. Therefore, to see what in actual practice political science will make of it, let me cite an example.

A concentration camp is, for the Nazis who institute it, a political institution. For the 6 million Jews who suffer it, it is a bare natural catastrophe. For the Jews it is perfectly indistinguishable from the onset of a pestilence, or of a famine, or of a holocaust, from the whole range of natural calamities which, since they cannot be imputed to any determinate responsible agency, we describe in the curiously cynical legal phrase as "acts of God." The Nazis who institute the camp stand opposite to one another in political relations. Their purpose is abominable. It is nevertheless, as they view it who find themselves obliged to the performance of the acts essential to advancing it, a common purpose, which suffices to unite them in a common undertaking. And in the measure that they conspire in that undertaking, and ally themselves under covenant in order to advance it, consenting to the mutual obligations which it requires, they preserve political relations as "I" and "Thou" to one another.

But with respect to the Jews whom they hold captive and labor to incinerate, they have, strictly, no political relationship whatever. The Jews they have put beyond their covenant, excluded from their society, degraded from the status of persons (subjects of rights) to the status of bare things (objects of rights, objects for use or abuse beyond capacity for rights) in the natural order. The Jews may stand under covenant rela-

tions with one another. But just as the Nazis sustain no political but only natural relations with them, so they, the remnant of Israel, are not politically related to the Nazis, but stand opposite to them, in naked encounter, beyond any shared covenant, in a state of nature.

Such is their circumstance as they see their circumstance who participate in it. Nazi is related to Nazi, and Jew to Jew, as person to person. But Nazi is related to Jew, and Jew to Nazi, as person to thing. How does political science describe these relations? It describes them all alike as relations of thing to thing. That is to say, it is wrong in all cases. It has grasped the abstract equilibrium that is the fact of nature; but it has ignored the political relapse, the eclipse of civility, that is the fact of history. It has therefore suspended the very distinction that to the participants in the event is regarded as the pivot of tragedy, the distinction between relations *de iure,* in which rights and duties may be acknowledged, and relations merely *de facto,* in which, in the absence of any shared covenant, rights and duties are without meaning or place or incidence.

Political science commits what I have elsewhere described as *the fallacy of the unimplicated spectator.*[6] It does not err in what it describes, for it describes exactly what it permits itself to see. But it describes only what is available to the perception of an external observer, to a spectator who is not party to the event described. It describes the fact of neighborhood, which belongs to nature, not the political achievement or the political deprivation, which belongs to history. The omission is critical. It is the disastrous omission that has caused the behavioral sciences, in all that concerns our social relations, to be blind to the fact of covenant in human life and to the meaning of civilization in the moral education of mankind.

The fallacy of the unimplicated spectator does not arise from an accident of oversight which a subsequent observation may correct. The fallacy is not a fault of negligence; it is a fault of perspective, systematic and methodical, which forbids us to study the most decisive aspects of our social encounter.

A behavioral science of society—any science that method-

ically suspends the point of view of the implicated observer—
will inevitably confuse force with authority, the dispensation
of ecology with the dispensation of law. If I may express the
matter quite generally, it confuses *order* with *rules of order*. The
consequence is the scandal of all positivism in our century.
We disqualify ourselves by prescription from distinguishing
grex from *humanitas,* herd from moral community, the condition of men in a state of nature from the condition of men in
a civil order of society.

When the *Mayflower* pilgrims, "solemnly and mutually in
the Presence of God and one another," made their compact,
promising submission and obedience to such laws and ordinances as from time to time should be thought convenient for
the general good, they constituted a society, they created "a
civil Body Politick," in a wilderness where none was, or at
least where none was believed to be. The laws and ordinances
had still to be framed as the exigencies of planting a colony
and providing for its permanent health and order made the
need for them manifest. But before any such enactments could
acquire the force of law, before any officer could speak with
the authority of the group, before any duty could be accounted
binding as an obligation on the member, this act was necessary. The Mayflower Compact is not a constitution; it is but
the preamble of a constitution whose body is unwritten. It
nevertheless records an act that is essential to civilized community in any of its forms. Into the herd we are all born in
pure passion; into our community, if we achieve community
at all, we are, as Nicodemus came to understand, reborn, reborn by our own act, into a new creation of our own.

Modern philosophy is said to begin with that strange
proposition of Descartes, *Cogito, ergo sum* ("I think, therefore
I am"). Social philosophy, if it begins with that proposition,
will be condemned to remain with it. For that proposition is
the prison of modern philosophy, and even Descartes was able
to escape its desolating solipsism only by forgetting the merciful malice of his demon. The first principle of social philosophy is not the proposition, "I think, therefore I am," but the

infinitely stranger proposition, *Es, et tu ipse, ergo sum,* which means, being interpreted, *"Thou* art, therefore I am."

In that simple perception is the sum of all civilization. The inheritance of civilization is not a matter of sentiment and old gold. Its austere task is the discovery of our moral community.

NOTES

1. *The Works of Francis Bacon,* collected and edited by James Spedding, Robert Leslie Ellis, and Douglas Denon Heath (Cambridge: Hurd and Houghton, 1869), vol. VIII, p. 53.

2. Immanuel Kant, *Foundations of the Metaphysics of Morals,* translated by Lewis White Beck (New York: Bobbs-Merrill, 1959), p. 34.

3. *Leviathan,* XVII.

4. Kant, op. cit., p. 47.

5. Martin Buber, *I and Thou,* translated by Ronald Gregor Smith, 2d. ed. (New York: Charles Scribner's Sons, 1958).

6. John F. A. Taylor, *The Masks of Society, An Inquiry into the Covenants of Civilization* (New York: Appleton-Century-Crofts, 1966), pp. 25–27, 66–73, 137–142.

7.

GENERAL
EDUCATION

An education suited to our season must be founded on a New
Instauration which does for the idea of Covenant in history
what Bacon did for the idea of Path in nature.

1. THE SOCIAL IMPLICATIONS OF THE HUMANITIES

It must be admitted by any impartial observer of the American
scene that the humanities do not in practice exercise the decisive influence that has been claimed for them. They color our
speech, they shape our observances, they temper our manners. Our institutions and our policy they leave unaffected.

The fault is not in them but in us. For we have never effectively permitted the humanities to demonstrate their critical
power as civilizing agencies in human life. "Dead things with
inbreath'd sense able to pierce," John Milton called them.
Such they are, but their critical value is registered only in pri-

vate appreciation. Their social implications—their significance for transforming the aims of education, the spirit of the market, and the objects of government—pass unspoken, unstudied, and even for the most part unreflected on. Our civilization has become in all of its major manifestations corporate. We have permitted our culture to become, as Marx described it, an idle superstructure and soliloquy.

Such is the typical arrest that we encounter amid the forms of modern industrial society. The ideals to which we subscribe, the values to which we educate our young, suppose a form of society in which men stand directly related to each other in independent dignity as person to person. In our actual society we stand indirectly related to each other through the multiplied corporations by which our roles are defined. In nation, in university, in business, in all of the decisive exchanges of our lives, the identity of the individual has been obscured by his corporate estate. We walk in anonymity, estranged by the hierarchies in which we meet and pass each other by. The individual has been lost in the member, the person in the functionary. The man in the welder's mask has become the image of our society. He sees himself as a human being; we see him in the nameless seclusion of his employments. The consequence is that, for him and for us, the ideals we teach are no longer clearly relevant to the lives we actually lead.

Thomas Carlyle once affirmed that if ever he had a sermon to preach, it would consist simply of this: "You people know what you ought to do; well, go out and do it!" His mother, who sat by, replied quietly: "Ay, Tammas, an' will ye tell them how?"

She speaks for all of us. For that surely is the question, how under the conditions of modern life to renew the meaning of old covenants, to restore the connection between old verity and new fact, in the ordered freedom of our society.

Christianity in its traditional forms supposes all moral relations to run between persons, and persons it conceives to correspond to natural individuals, like you and me. In our world, that simple correspondence can no longer be assumed. The decisive contemporary persons are not individuals at all; they are collectivities, corporations, nations—artificial entities which we have contrived, by convention, in the face of nature. Where they are not, their decisions are not those that in fact structure our society.

In such a world the Judaeo-Christian command to love one's neighbor as oneself is not without meaning; it is simply without intelligible application. What can it mean to love my neighbor as myself if General Motors is my neighbor, Mc-Donald's my innkeeper, and Fisher Body my bunkmate? And if I am forbidden to suppose nations capable of mutuality, capable of reciprocal obligations and reciprocal respect for rights, then the peace of nations is a delusion, and the conflict of nations an incorrigible datum of the human world.

Let Russia contract to buy wheat from the United States. The parties to the exchange are nation-states; there is no sovereign beyond them to enforce the terms of civility into which they have entered. Each party to the contract exchanges a right to what it gives for the right to what it gets. Getting and giving, both parties subscribe to a tacit covenant which underlies their spoken contract and logically precedes it, that each is to be regarded for that occasion (if only for that occasion) as a person, that is, in the language of the law, as a subject of rights. Voluntarily, they consent to meet in good faith as equals in a temporary community of exchange, each party acknowledging a right to lie in the other, each laying an obligation upon itself. Their community is a fiction? It is by such unspoken fictions that their peace (and yours and mine) is maintained.

The error of our times is to dignify the balance of power and to make the consent to a community of nations superfluous. We have put Leviathan beyond covenant, corporations beyond civility, and ourselves beyond each other. But if Israel, which was a nation, can make covenants in Sinai, then why should Russia or General Motors be thought a beast in the wilderness?

When Aristotle wrote his *Politics,* he understood as well

as any modern author, and more sensibly than some, that the perfected development of the human individual is not realizable apart from society, apart from corporate community, apart from the duties and consecrations of a common life. The birth of the free individual was nevertheless, as he conceived, the justification of all society, the discipline of all intercourse, the end and object of all government. Why, then, should that affirmation, which is the essential burden of the whole humanistic tradition of the Western world, have become so untenable in our day? The reason is clear. We think still according to the immemorial stereotypes of an old dispensation, framing in our industrial and metropolitan civilization an education that fits men only for the Greek *polis* or for the agrarian society of Jefferson.

The default of humanistic education in the modern world has never been that it has failed to transmit the undefiled vision of Christianity or of Greece. Its scholarship has not been unequal to its commission. Its default lies in the systematic assumption that the purity of the transmitted ideal is sufficient to the needs of the hour. It is not. In the life of animals inheritance is a datum; in the life of human beings it is always a task. To every generation the task remains of reworking its covenants, of reestablishing their meaning and relevance for men and women who do and suffer, live and act, in the birth of a new creation.

This liability is the great recurrent theme of the tragic poets. "Is man no more than this?" asks King Lear in the last extremity of moral desolation as he beholds Edgar naked and shivering in the lash of the storm (III, iv). "Thou owest the worm no silk, the beast no hide, the sheep no wool, the cat no perfume. . . . Thou art the thing itself: unaccommodated man is no more but such a poor, bare, forkt animal as thou art."

What is the difference between "accommodated" and "unaccommodated" man? It is the difference between existence in the shelter of moral community and existence beyond it. Beyond community the human creature is a bare animal in nature; in community he becomes a person in history. And the accommodation transfigures him. By consent to the terms of community he is delivered out of the bondage of mere nature, enters into the human estate, and is clothed with the dignity of a moral subject.

A child speaks in the language of its parents. The child as it is born into the world has already its capacity for speech. But this formal capacity that belongs to the child at birth is essentially incomplete. It is not merely undeveloped; it is radically indeterminate. The child's capacity can be realized only within the historically specific conventions of a language, and these conventions—the conventions, for example, of English or of French, of Chinese or of Russian—remain still for the child to discover. The education of the child to the power of symbolism is always therefore in the first instance an exercise of midwifery, the release of a natural capacity which the child has without benefit of education. But the matrix of language into which the child is received is a historical structure that evolves according to its own laws by human institution. Nature does not afford it; the child does not invent it; education does but transmit it as one of the forms of community the child is ready to receive. Such forms, as Aristotle used to say, come neither by nature nor against nature; but nature gives the capacity for acquiring them, and this capacity is developed by training. Let the bare capacity for speech be described as the child's first nature, then the ruleful exercise of that capacity within the constraints of an already instituted language may be described as its second nature. In every historical domain— in language, in art, in science, in religion, in politics, in economy—education is the development and cultivation of such a second nature. Whatever is distinctive of accommodated man, whatever is his by entitlement of humanity, belongs to him by education, that is to say, by inheritance or by institution, in the human estate.[1]

2. PROCESS-VALUES

Wherever human beings ally themselves in voluntary society, they design to reconcile freedom and order in their relations to each other. They cannot live without order; they will not live without freedom. Therefore, the achievement of civility in human affairs presents always the same paradox. What human beings essentially want in their voluntary associations is an *ordered freedom*—a freedom to pursue their own purposes without interference so long as they respect the conditions necessary to their common life. The conditions necessary to their common life are the restraints that the members of a free society voluntarily lay upon themselves, in order that they might frame normal expectations of each other. Any freedom which is not attended with that measure of order is delusive; any order which is not attended with that measure of freedom is impermanent.

The covenant of a free society must be renewed in every generation, and it is this recurrent demand, unwaivable in a free society, that sets the path of education. Only in a society that understands the conditions of its own renewal is an ordered freedom possible. That is why the central problem of free society in our times is the discovery of the meaning of general education.

If we had the spontaneous objectivity of the Greeks in reflecting upon our social institutions, we should describe general education, as Aristotle describes the state,[2] as a "natural institution"—*paideia kata physin*. In Aristotle's conception of politics there are conditions of civility that lie beyond the vicissitudes of mere human convention. The difference between the laws of the Athenians and the laws of the Spartans is an artificial variation which the Greeks ascribed to Solon and Lykurgus. These framers of constitutions had different conceptions of human society—different "ideologies" or "paradigms," as we nowadays would say; therefore each legislated in order to realize his special vision of the social good. But beneath these differences, which belong to history, there are, says Aristotle, conditions of civility that belong to nature, which underlie the establishment of the peace of human community as such, and without which there can be neither peace nor any distinctively human society whatever. The natural conditions of civility are not an incident of contract or convention; they are the objective conditions that are indispensably necessary if we are to meet and voluntarily abide as equals in one assembly. Any establishment of law, any system of artificial conventions, that runs counter to these natural conditions of human society will be found corrupt, impermanent, and self-defeating.

In Aristotle's understanding of the term "nature," general education could be simply and very accurately defined as an education *according to nature* (*kata physin*). But the term "nature" has in modern usage changed its meaning, and this simplicity of idiom is denied to us. Our modern conception of nature is drawn not from Aristotle but from Darwin. The human drama unfolds itself upon a neutral stage. The stage sets the inexorable limits of any play that may be performed upon it, but it leaves the play itself unwritten. In nature there is process but no due process, order but no rule of order, history but no mandate. Displacement alone is natural; all else is artificial, arbitrary, merely conventional, since nature has no direction of its own. The simple consequence of the theory of natural selection is precisely that nature selects nothing. Nature establishes no covenant, takes no side, shows no favor, in the fierce contests which we wage within it. The strong survive, not because nature favors strength, but because, nature favoring nothing, the weak are eliminated. Therefore, in the moral vacuity of Darwin's universe, no one thinks to ask the pivotal question that concerns us all, Whether the human drama which nature leaves unwritten has not conditions of its own, formal conditions without which there could be no play at all?

Let us ask that question: What formal conditions are we obliged to institute if we would realize, in our relations to each other, the ordered freedom of a voluntary society capable of renewing itself? The possibility of a general education rests upon the answer we give to this question. We need to develop the idea of a consensual system that is in principle self-correcting.

To describe its opposition to the governing party in English political life, the minority in the British Parliament entitles itself "Her Majesty's loyal opposition." To an Englishman the idea of a loyal opposition flows directly from constitutional principle. The systematic criticism of public policy is a function essential to free government. The loyal opposition is not an alien interruption of the public tranquility; it is one of the conditions of the public tranquility, a positive public office, an office as indefeasible in the system of English government as the formal ministries occupied by the party in power. The right of the minority to be heard or, what is the same thing, the duty of the majority to hear it, may be inconvenient, cumbrous, even at times politically perilous. It nevertheless secures this permanent benefit, that the English system of government provides for the peaceful transformation of itself. The system is self-correcting. The right of the loyal opposition runs always against the majority in power, which is temporary, never against the system (or, as the English prefer to say, "the majesty of the crown"), which is reverable, continuous, and permanent.

The idea of a loyal opposition lies at the foundation of the peace of a democratic society. A democratic society harbors all of the collisions of interest that belong to any other form of society. But it is the one form of political organization that is in principle self-correcting. Beyond all of the temporary displacements of power that are registered in majorities, it alone undertakes to secure that the public councils remain permanently open, hospitable to the variations of sentiment and opinion that are the inevitable accompaniments of free community. By the neutrality of its process a democratic society shelters the public argument and consents to be led by it. The path of the society will be at any time determined by the decision of a majority. But only the right of an open dissent can illuminate the alternative paths the majority has failed to take; and the freedom of the society depends on the active preservation of these live alternatives.

I call any consensual system which is thus in principle

self-correcting a *process-value*. Any system that by providing for the peaceful transformation of itself reconciles freedom with authority, change with continuity, and conflict with resolutions commonly agreed upon will satisfy this condition. Parliamentary government is simply the grandest and most familiar example. But there are others equally demonstrable in every major domain of civilization. The peace of the market viewed as a voluntary community of exchange is a process-value; the growth of the common law under judicial interpretation is a process-value; what Tillich used to describe as "the Protestant principle" in religious community is a process-value. Wherever decisions are governed by rules of order that define due process in the common consent, there, for those who are party to the consent, process-values are in operation. Process-values are the content of general education.

The covenant of the university is a process-value. In the peaceful exchanges of the scientific community we witness an illustration (in practice the purest illustration that we know) of a self-correcting system transmitting itself according to rules of due process from generation to generation.

The university is, however, a community of criticism, not of doctrine. It will not tell us what to believe; it tells us only the limits of warranted belief. What, then, in the absence of doctrine, is left for the university to teach? I answer very simply: the conditions of our intellectual and moral community, the terms of peace under covenant in every domain of civilized activity, including its own.

That is not a description of our practice. American practice in higher education oscillates between a totally elective curriculum and a curriculum totally prescribed. A totally elective curriculum has this great disadvantage, that it leaves the most weighty and important decisions to the parties least informed. Students are expected in the name of abstract freedom to frame their own programs, improvising on matters of gravest consequence before which even their wisest mentors would hesitate. A totally prescribed curriculum makes the contrary error. It takes the decision concerning the values to be sought in education out of the hands of those who must endure the penalties of error. Distribution programs attempt to discover a middle path. The student is free to choose among restricted ranges of options that distribute benefits (e.g., in natural science, social science, and humanities) according to proportions set by the faculty. There are many such programs. All of them agree in assuming that generality in education consists in an exposure to the established departments of learning and research. All assume, in short, that generality is a matter of path not of covenant.

In May, 1978, by a vote of 182 to 65, the faculty of arts and sciences of Harvard University approved a new curriculum for Harvard undergraduates.[3] The "Core Curriculum," as the new scheme was called, was the formal recommendation of a committee specially charged to review Harvard's general education program. The existing program, now in process of being displaced, had governed the pattern of undergraduate education since World War II, and there was wide agreement that the original purposes for which it had been instituted were no longer served. Students were asked to choose among the courses that might happen to be offered by the general education committee in any given year. Except for distribution requirements, a student's selection was virtually unrestricted. "Our regulations," wrote Dean Henry Resovsky, "do not carry the conviction that there are any agreed-upon priorities." The restitution of such priorities was the object of any responsible reform of undergraduate education.

The new curriculum is a deliberate effort to restore design to undergraduate education, shaping requirements so as to produce, by premeditation, the basic literacy of an educated person. "Degree requirements," says the *Report*, "are the standards—the *minimum* standards—of higher education. Individuals may exceed [these] standards, but they are not at liberty to fall below them. . . . The critical task is to justify a particular set of requirements . . . on intellectual grounds." Under the new plan students will be permitted to spend the equivalent of one academic year (one of the total of four) in courses freely chosen. The elective principle has not been suspended; it has been simply circumscribed, given its proper place, in the fabric of a Harvard education. The restitution of priorities is announced in two sets of requirements—the general requirements of a core curriculum and the special requirements of a field of concentration. The two sets of requirements are complementary; both are essential; for the purposes of general education at Harvard they are now, by prescription, inseparable. The concentration requirements provide for depth in some field of knowledge; the nonconcentration requirements provide for "a basic literacy in major forms of intellectual discourse." The two sets conjoined are meant to produce "a solid and shared base" of education for all students.

When at commencement ceremonies the Harvard faculty welcomes a student "to the company of educated men and women," what in fact, beyond technical accomplishment in a major field, does it mean? It means, in the terms of the *Report,* the core curriculum. The core curriculum is, in the committee's own description, "an amalgam." Every student is obliged to demonstrate a proficiency in expository writing, a basic knowledge of mathematics through algebra, and a reading competence in a foreign language. These preliminary requirements being satisfied, every student is required to take from seven to ten courses (in total the equivalent of one academic year) in five "core areas" representing different "intellectual approaches" and major "substantive areas of knowledge":

Literature and the Arts,
History,
Social and Philosophical Analysis,
Science and Mathematics,
Foreign Languages and Cultures.

As in all such undertakings, everything depends on what will in fact be done within this formal scheme. The definition of core areas is not likely to disturb the slumber of professionals. The fault of the Harvard curriculum is not that it requires a distribution of content; its fault is that the content distributed remains as specialized after distribution as it was before. You do not mend a civilization by moving furniture. The new curriculum does but illustrate, redundantly, the omission it was designed to remedy. It betrays our persistent incapacity to focus on process-values, the self-correcting systems that underlie and regulate free institutions wherever men and women are equal to the peace of civilization. If I ask myself whether an educated person can afford to be ignorant of one or another of Harvard's five core areas, I reply that the members of the Harvard faculty have for years, without detection, managed to do so. But if I ask whether an educated person can afford to be ignorant of the Harvard faculty's covenant of inquiry, that is, of the due process of verification and explanation under commonly admitted rules of evidence, I reply that no educated person can.

3. GENERAL EDUCATION

The detachment that enables the university to span generations and nations, tribes and classes, jurisdictions and legacies, disqualifies it for the limited partisanships that belong to society's ordinary actors. Shelter of competing ideologies, it is not itself an ideology. On the contrary, the university is the sustained critical effort to organize a community of belief under the rules of an open process. It ranges before us, in the search for the peace of human community, all contests, all paradigms of science and patterns of culture, all of the significant options in the history of civilization. How, then, without partisanship among these options, shall it educate? By making of partisanship itself a *critical* problem.

No one has spoken so wisely on this matter as Michel de Montaigne, who was content to write simply of the education of children:

The tutor should make his pupil sift everything, and take nothing into his head on simple authority or trust. Aristotle's principles must no more be principles with him than those of the Stoics or the Epicureans. Let their various opinions be put before him; he will choose between them if he can; if not, he will remain in doubt. Only fools are certain and immovable. . . . The bees steal from this flower and that, but afterwards turn their pilferings into honey, which is their own; it is thyme and marjoram no longer.[4]

The critical problem of education is how to make thyme and marjoram one's own.

When at age sixteen I entered the university, I was firmly of opinion that the advancement of learning could take place only in Gothic buildings. Of that opinion (as of other innocence) I was quickly disabused. The campus displayed on every hand a borrowed splendor of cloister and carillon, arched entranceways and studiously gloomy corridors, ribbed vaults and massy buttresses, crockets, legends in stained glass, and a whole bestiary of carved gargoyles that made roof water amusing. Everyone secretly delighted in the outward solemnity of this façade that the Gothic afforded; but it was considered unforgivably rude to betray this secret. Fashionable opinion required that you deprecate in public what pleased your soul in private. So in those days you lived Gothic Revival and spoke pure Bauhaus. Was it not regrettable (you were taught to ask) that the whole of this array, grand as it seemed and undeniably impressive as it was, was sham, a monumental sham, that anyone could purchase for the price of an ornament? Had we no forms that were cognate to the unexplored possibilities of modern materials and techniques, no forms that were equal to expressing our new surmise and proper dignity? Divorced from these demands, architecture was but stage scenery, a fake backdrop against which we dramatized a learned pretense. We trafficked in Gothic forms without running Gothic risks. Everybody knew that these bell towers, which appeared to scratch the sky and seemed so daring, were reinforced with steel bars embedded in concrete. And I remember my shock at learning, when I admired the interior of Saint Patrick's Cathedral in New York, that its great vaults, which I took to be a miracle of flight in terms of tons of gravitating stone, in fact consisted of *papier-mâché*. If it is permissible to lie even in a house of God, then surely it is permissible to lie on the Princeton campus. The trouble with Neo-Gothic (as with Neo-Classic or Neo-Bauhaus) is not in the forms inherited; the trouble is in the manner of inheritance, which treats the forms as incorrigibly final, as merely imitable, therefore as usable only by the lately dead.

Let it be asked, What actually do we *mean* when in the Western tradition we speak of the legacy of Greece or Rome, of Israel or Christianity? Well, we mean of course, for one thing, scrolls, manuscripts, and old stones—the shattered Parthenon, faded parchments, frayed pieces of papyrus. But invariably we mean more than that, and anyone who understood us to mean only that would have mistaken our serious intent. He would have confused treasure with vessel, the essential patrimony with the outward vehicle in which patrimony is preserved.[5] Indispensably we require a distinction to be drawn between *the physically inherited forms,* which are present and manifest but fragmentary, and the *informing principle,* which is latent and implicit but whole. Thus we say of the Doric order of the Parthenon that it may be borrowed or imitated or stolen, as one wears a borrowed ornament. But we say of the informing principle of the Parthenon that it cannot be borrowed, it must be rethought, as one discovers a buried power.

What do we in fact inherit in the Parthenon? The question is ambiguous, since physically we inherit one thing, historically another. Physically, we inherit the empty building, the majestic remnant, the ordered (and disordered) thing of stone; historically, we inherit, in Henry James's phrase, its "felt life," the style of mind that ordered it and may be read out of it. The answer we choose will depend on the kind of apprehension, active or passive, that we bring to it. If we apprehend the Parthenon passively, we see the vacated utility, the physical residue disused, that may be put to use, or left unused, according to present accidents and instant purposes. We see without historical imagination or empathy, as the Turk saw who stored his ammunition there, or as the Venetian Morosini saw who fired upon it and destroyed it. But if we apprehend the Parthenon actively, we discover in the empty shell of the building, besides ruins, an intimation of persons. We discover, in spite of brokenness and disorder, the immanent design which accident has disturbed but failed to obliterate—a canon of proportions, a rule of order, the objectification of a style of mind, to which human beings, living men and women, once freely consented, and in which they found expression, in the unborrowed sufficiency of their common life. And it is this objectified style of mind—not the relic thing but the covenant of persons implicit in it—that is the essential patrimony, the living testament, of the Parthenon.

Pericles called the covenant of Athens the "school of Hellas." And it was surely that. All that was germinal and original in the Greek sense of community was accomplished in the Athenian experience; and all who would learn of Hellas must learn first of Athens, in whose institutions—in whose architecture and sculpture and poetry, philosophy and drama and history—its genius was most perfectly consummated.

Why is not the covenant of Athens the school also of America? For the reason that a generation can enter into its patrimony only by transforming it. Each generation inherits according to the forms it brings to its inheritance. A generation that brings nothing inherits nothing. For each works, as Athens in its time was obliged to work and as America now works, out of its own historical situation. The historical situation of Athens was as specific and untransferable as ours, and Athens rose to meet it in its own terms. What Pericles meant by Hellas was the Athenian resolution of a special historical problem. Only the style of mind that animated it is its generalizable pure bequest. But it is we, not Hellas, who must generalize it, who must discover how to extend it, beyond the limits of the Greek idiom, in a new idiom of our own.

That transformation is what general education is about. General education does not begin with accomplished generalities. It begins with the search for informing principle. Generality is its aim, not its origin. Anyone blind to the new possibilities of Classical design in steel cantilevers and glass and poured concrete must be equally blind to the spirit of Classical design in the marble posts and lintels of the Parthenon. Our young must be taught to see that the Classical spirit transcends the Greek idiom, the Greek ideology, the Greek imagination, the Greek predicament. In the modern predicament the Classical spirit has nothing to do with the revival of the Greek orders; it consists in a renewal of the Greek principle, in a renewal of the generalized demand for restraint, for intelligible simplicity, for perspicuously ordered proportions, in *any* context. The Neo-Classic slumbers with the borrowed form that is settled and incorrigible; the Classic respects the informing principle, the process-value, that is open to development, still to be traversed, and permanently problematic. The right use of Athens in the contemporary scene is not a new Athens but a new America.

And the same is true of all of the historically achieved options of human community. It is not enough that we should take from Greece or Rome, or from Israel or Christianity, or from all of these and others together, the finished pattern of American civilization. It is not enough even if we could. But we cannot. The regret of Gerontion grown old, to whom the gods granted eternal life but denied eternal youth, images the failure of historicism in all of its adventures.

> After such knowledge, what forgiveness? Think now
> History has many cunning passages, contrived corridors
> And issues, deceives with whispering ambitions,
> Guides us by vanities. Think now
> She gives when our attention is distracted
> And what she gives, gives with such supple confusions
> That the giving famishes the craving. Gives too late
> What's not believed in, or if still believed,
> In memory only, reconsidered passion.[6]

We inherit contrary covenants—covenants of science, covenants of religion, all of the manifold covenants of civilization that history has produced but failed to reconcile. We inherit them, moreover, in a world whose specific problems are alien to Athens, alien to Rome, alien to Israel or to Christianity.

Therefore, as we would take up our inheritance, we are obliged to work at it, to construct in order to reconstruct, to transform in order properly to venerate. A common inheritance does not produce community but, on the contrary, presupposes it.

4. OF TEACHING AND LEARNING

If I give to my son my father's watch, it must appear to any observer unimplicated in the event that the transmission is completed with the transfer. My son now wears the watch my father wore and that I have worn after him. But for the persons implicated in the event—for the father and the son—that description, though it notes the external transfer of the watch, ignores the moral significance of the event, the significance of a consent to covenant that is the paramount fact in the understanding of the participants. The meaning they apprehend and have chosen thus outwardly to celebrate is the moral union of the generations that inherit and bequeathe. The subscription to covenant—not the wearing of the watch, but the affirmation of the community of those who wear it, or have worn it, or will wear it—is the moral meaning of the act, its meaning as the participants understand its meaning even before the physical transfer has been made. The watch has become the visible outward sign of the ligature, unbroken and invisible, that binds their generations, accusing and excusing, to each other.

Such is the peculiarity of all education, if it succeeds. The parties to the transfer—the generation that gives and the generation that receives—are, and conceive themselves to be, parties to the covenant that is conveyed by it. Education is in this sense always public, a consecration of persons to the obligations of a common life. It is for the persons party to it an act, not merely of transfer, but of union. The bare physical transfer is ambiguous; the covenant that enables us to interpret it is not. The difference will pass unnoticed when education succeeds; when education fails, it is society's stark register that the generations are estranged. The inheriting generation absconds with its patrimony; the bequeathing generation throws it away.

The real genius of the Socratic dialogue eludes us. It eludes us even as it eluded his contemporaries at the threshold of the Western tradition. The genius of the dialogue lies in Socrates' heroic discovery that the argument leads him, not he it. He yields to the demonstration as submissively as his hearers. For the connections he brings forward are, like those in a geometer's proof, not arbitrary connections. They do not bind us to a conclusion because they have chanced to be spoken by a person in authority or heard by persons who are prepared even without argument to consent to his opinions. On the contrary, the authority of the teacher is as independent of him as of them. His claim to authority is admissible solely for the reason that he accedes to standards of argument that are already commonly admitted, in tacit consent, before the argument is spoken or heard.

There is a regrettable egotism that it has been our habit to cultivate in students. We cultivate in them the belief that the conquest of learning depends on their sentimental satisfaction with the process. Students—especially students in America—object to learning anything except by actual discussion. Their instinct is unassailably healthy. They mistrust preachment; they refuse to be passively indoctrinated. But they mistakenly suppose that the demand for discussion, for confronting both sides of an argument, requires all parties to speak. They suppose that a lecture in which their responses are not respectfully solicited and heard is waste motion, the lecturer's soliloquy, not the student's advance. They are therefore baffled to discover themselves, on occasion, profoundly instructed by a lecture in which they have spoken not a word.

What in fact has happened? The lecturer has spoken for them, not only for himself but for them as well. Selflessly and without constraint, he has spoken for all who would hear and be party to the argument he recites. He has spoken prophetically as the prophets spoke who appeared out of the hills, declaring in the terms of a covenant already shared what all knew but none so clearly understood.

The teacher stands opposite to his student, who is seen; but he stands also opposite to his professional peers, who normally are not seen but whose presence is nevertheless registered in the due process of his act. This complication of the teacher's role, that he performs not merely an individual but a representative act, normally escapes his immediate addressees. For the student responds focally to the thrust of the discourse. He attends critically to the conduct of the argument, not to the person (either himself or the teacher) who is party to it. Such is the peculiarity of the teaching and learning relation. The standard of argument, the demand for evidence that presides for both the teacher and the student, is independent of the material circumstance that it is they and not others who argue; or that it is the teacher and not the student who expounds; or that it is the student and not the teacher for whose benefit, for the most part, the argument takes place. And this is the profoundly social fact that we have by long habit neglected, namely, that the act of teaching or of learning presupposes the community of scholars. Very simply, it presupposes the dialogue of the university. It presupposes the singularity of the covenant of inquiry, the tacit consent on the part of all inquirers to a rule of due process which we may describe, in the idiom of Émile Durkheim, as a *conscience collective.* Teaching is not the simple binary relation of a teacher and a student. It is the common participation of both in a community that extends beyond either of them and transcends the material conditions of their encounter.

The task of general education is not the task of conquering the land or settling the frontier. The land has been conquered; the frontier has been settled. The task now is to rediscover the city beneath the asphalt. God had it easier on creation day. He worked from nothing, therefore had nothing to erase or accommodate. In the design of cities, on the contrary, the educator works always on a muddy slate. He works, as an architect works, inevitably from what is given, from all that is generous in our promise, from all that is inhumane, remediable but unremedied, in our fact. The modern educator's problem is the rational ordering of a peopled space, in which our functions and our practices are assembled and made humanly intelligible, in one design. And that requires of us, in education as in architecture, a new kind of social vision, which studies how to organize variety without extinguishing it, how to reconcile our privacy with our independence, how to restore a positive relationship between our work and our leisure, how not merely to serve needs but to teach us, in Woodrow Wilson's phrase, "the lure of things worthy to be loved."

NOTES

1. Pico della Mirandola, who stands between the medieval dispensation and the humanism of the Renaissance, declares the singularity of our moral circumstance in the *Oration on the Dignity of Man*. God says to Adam: "We have made thee neither of heaven nor of earth, neither mortal nor immortal, so that with freedom of choice . . . , as though the maker and molder of thyself, thou mayest fashion thyself in whatever shape thou shalt prefer. Thou shalt have the power to degenerate into the lower forms of life, which are brutish. Thou shalt have the power out of thy soul's judgment to be reborn into the higher forms, which are divine." *The Renaissance Philosophy of Man,* selections in translation, edited by Ernst Cassirer, Paul Oskar Kristeller, and John Herman Randall, Jr. (Chicago: University of Chicago Press, 1948), p. 225.

2. *The Politics of Aristotle, Translated with an Analysis and Critical Notes by J. E. C. Welldon* (London: Macmillan, 1893), I, ii, 5.

3. The "Report on Harvard's 'Core Curriculum' " is reprinted in *The Chronicle of Higher Education,* (March 6, 1978), pp. 1, 15–19. The approval of the report is announced, with accompanying commentaries, in *The Chronicle of Higher Education,* (May 8, 1978), p. 1, 12.

4. Michel de Montaigne, *Essays, Translated with an Introduction by J. M. Cohen* (Baltimore: Penguin Books, 1958 [1966]), p. 56.

5. Cf., above, p. 52.

6. T. S. Eliot, *Gerontion,* ll. 33–41.

INDEX